Liu Sanjie

Her Free and Undying
Mountain Songs

刘三姐歌谣英译与演唱

（汉英对照）

黄少政 / 编译

Compiled and Translated
by Huang Shaozheng

GUANGXI NORMAL UNIVERSITY PRESS
广西师范大学出版社
·桂林·

刘三姐歌谣英译与演唱
LIU SANJIE GEYAO YINGYI YU YANCHANG

图书在版编目（CIP）数据

刘三姐歌谣英译与演唱：汉英对照／黄少政编译. ——
桂林：广西师范大学出版社，2021.8
ISBN 978-7-5598-4103-2

Ⅰ．①刘… Ⅱ．①黄… Ⅲ．①歌舞剧－剧本－作品
集－中国－当代－汉、英 Ⅳ．①I233

中国版本图书馆 CIP 数据核字（2021）第 150019 号

广西师范大学出版社出版发行

（广西桂林市五里店路 9 号 邮政编码：541004）
网址：http://www.bbtpress.com
出版人：黄轩庄
全国新华书店经销
广西民族印刷包装集团有限公司印刷
（南宁市高新区高新三路 1 号 邮政编码：530007）
开本：880 mm × 1 240 mm 1/32
印张：8 字数：210 千
2021 年 8 月第 1 版 2021 年 8 月第 1 次印刷
定价：58.00 元

如发现印装质量问题，影响阅读，请与出版社发行部门联系调换。

谨以本书向近七十年来，呕心沥血、群策群力，将刘三姐打造成为壮乡广西首席代言人的编剧、编曲、表演艺术家及其他文艺工作者致敬。他们的杰出贡献，携天籁般的刘三姐歌谣，为八桂五千万儿女增辉，与旖旎秀丽的岭南山水同美。

Dedicated to the brilliant cast of script writers, musicians, performing artists of Liu Sanjie in Liuzhou Caidiao Operas, films, and other works, whose sustained effort and wisdom, spanning nearly seven decades, has uplifted a marginalized legend, i.e., Liu Sanjie, an obscure Zhuang herorine, into the chief IP of Guangxi Zhuang Autonomous Region.

目　录

Contents

序

有一种爱叫山歌

马克·特雷迪尼克

一

相传在中国南方桂林城附近的喀斯特山区，生活过一位秀美的农家姑娘。她动人的歌喉婉转而又迷人，天地万物无不为之赞叹，山川、河流无不为之动容，令百鸟鸣啭黯然失色，精通音律者自叹弗如。她的美貌更令当地广有田产的土豪垂涎三尺，不惜高价雇用秀才在歌圩上与她一决高下。有人说，姑娘逃离了土豪的迫害，与恋人隐姓埋名，遁入了大山深处；更有传说，这对情人变成了两只鸣禽，这是他们为歌咏自由和爱情付出的代价。

这位壮族"歌仙"人称刘三姐，相传生活于公元8世纪初的唐朝。她在鱼峰山下唱过的歌谣和其他山歌都是即兴创作的。三姐秀外慧中、才情斐然，被壮族人奉为仙女，此后1300多年间，她的歌谣经口耳相传，经久不衰。她集山歌创作与演唱于一身，可谓前无古人，后无来者。

Preface

How to Love Like a Mountain

Mark Tredinnick

1

It is said that in the karst mountains near the city of Guilin in China's south, there once roamed a beautiful peasant girl, whose singing pleased the heavens and did justice to the beauty of the rivers and the fields and peaks and rivalled the birds and shamed the music scholars and seduced and outwitted an evil landlord. Some say she escaped the tyrant and lived out her days obscurely with her lover in the mountains. Other tellings turn them into two songbirds, the price they paid for their refusal to let the singing of her people be stilled.

She was Liu Sanjie ("Third Sister Liu"), or so she became called. She is said to have lived and sung, this angel of song, during the Tang dynasty, in the early years of the eighth century. Her people were the Zhuang, and her name has been held sacred and her songs have been sung among them these thirteen

即便这样的歌仙不曾真实存在，历史也一定会创造一个刘三姐。事实证明的确如此。这个姑娘和她的歌谣、短暂而极富诗意与英雄气概的一生，是所有时代都需要的养分，是人类精神赖以生存的神话。文学所为者何？不就是书写讴歌这样的平民英雄吗？而刘三姐的故事和歌谣经历代搜集、整理、传唱，终于汇集成了一种精致的民间歌谣文学。纵观人类历史，寄寓文学作品的"兴、观、群、怨"的种种主张和因此彰显的真、善、美，都在她的歌谣中一一得到了实践：她主持正义，谴责不公；在思想、精神和肉体层面她都拒绝屈服于任何权势，也绝不让我们屈服；她歌咏艰辛凡世中的点滴快乐，这种乐观的生活态度，凝结在歌声中化为永恒。她，一如所有高迈真诚的诗歌，是正义、美、爱与自由的化身。

刘三姐身处男权社会，又归属主流文化之外的边疆民族。她出身贫寒，每一天醒来就要为谋生而劳作，族人还饱受欺凌压迫。可她天生有一副好嗓子，虽身处边缘与委顿穷困，却唱出了鄙视强势话语的歌谣，对得之不义的财富嗤之以鼻，以一种罕见的决绝和自觉守护个体生命的自主和神圣，并向世界大声宣称：青春神圣，爱情神圣，年轻拥有随心而非随俗的权利。她歌颂了灵魂对世界的叛逆、自我对险境的反抗、底层对强权的斗争。

正因如此，刘三姐才称得上是独立女性，她的歌谣才称得上是文学，

hundred years since, for she is said to have performed the ballads of Yufeng Mountain, and the other mountain songs of her people, and to have improvised in that idiom, with a divine kind of grace and wit and intelligence. Hers was a talent for composition and performance of the songs of the mountains, the love songs of the earth, never rivalled, before or after.

If such a young woman never existed, history would have to have invented her, and to a large extent it has. She and her music and her short, lyric, heroic life story are the kind of thing all ages need, the kind of myth the human spirit depends upon. Third Sister what literature is for. No matter who co-opts her life and story and songs——and many have——Liu Sanjie made a small literature of folk music that does what literature, through human history, has always done, and which we need it to keep on doing: she insists on justice; she decries inequity; she refuses to be cowed, or to let us be cowed, in mind, spirit, and body; she transfigures everyday experience into small eternities of song. She stands, in other words, as all poetry of integrity does, for justice and beauty and love and freedom.

Liu Sanjie was a woman in a man's world. Hers was a minority culture. Her family was poor, and as a girl in a tenant-farming family, she had little to hope for from life; her mountain people were colonised and oppressed. She knew no privilege but the gift of her voice. She came from the edges; and from the edges and out of her poverty, she sang what all dominant discourses overlook or disparage: the autonomy and irreverent divinity of each human life, the right of each human heart to love what and whom and how it loves. Her songs sing the rebellion of the soul against the world, of the self against its unpropitious circumstances, of the marginalised against the powerful.

All that makes Liu Sanjie, the Third Sister Liu, a woman, and hers a

流芳千载，激励世人。刘三姐的这些歌谣，看似是自中古以来流传下来的民歌蓝本，在黄少政笔下被译为短小精练的现代英语文学作品后，更像是在我们这个时代创作出来的。刘三姐简直像是为我们这个时代而生的。当下，东西方的艺术文化学者都将目光投向少数民族文化、女性艺术、沉默群体、边缘群体和殖民地的诗歌，活在唐朝的刘三姐，这个南方大山里的壮族民谣歌者，也以女性之身，为我们的时代唱响赞歌。

时至今日，刘三姐仍是壮族人心中的神，是山野文化中正直、不羁与坚韧的象征。儒家学者将她塑造为一个音乐奇才，给她编配了一个出身上层的丈夫；年轻的新中国也打出她的旗帜，将她拥戴为人民英雄、反抗压迫的斗士、敢于智斗嘲弄旧知识分子的歌者。在以她名字命名的彩色电影中，刘三姐被刻画为人民的女儿、胆识过人的阶级战士。电影1961年上映时，在国内外大获成功，广受赞誉。其后，她成了壮族的标志，为广西的文化发展、民族融合做出了贡献。而如今，刘三姐成了国内外游客纷纷探访桂林的缘由之一，是仅次于桂林喀斯特地貌的广西第二大旅游热点，几个世纪以来，一直吸引着诗人、画家与朝圣者慕名前来。

隐于山野，天真未凿，年轻姑娘声如天籁，歌声不绝；山歌悠扬，即兴而成，所歌者何，歌为心声。

literature, for all times and all people. But more than ever, her small literature, translated here into clear contemporary English, is a folk poetry for our times. And her life could almost have been coined for these days——as art and cultural scholarship in both the east and the west give attention to minority cultures, to women's art, to silenced voices, to lives on the margins, to colonised lyrics. Liu Sanjie of the Tang Dynasty, Zhuang folk singer from the mountains of the south, stands as a woman, her songs as anthems, for our times.

For her people, Third Sister Liu was and remains a saint, a symbol of the integrity and sensuality and resilience of their mountain culture. Confucian scholars construed her as a prodigy and married her off to a noble. The young PRC recruited her as a heroine of the people, a champion of the oppressed, and used her as a stick to beat intellectuals with. It is as a darling of the masses, a spunky class warrior, that filmmakers depicted her the film that bears her name shot in technicolour and rolled out to a clamour of popular acclaim in 1961 in China and beyond. Later, she was rebranded as a Zhuang icon, to support a claim for Guangxi's special administrative status. These days, people from across China and the world travel to Guilin because of her. Among the reasons tourists come to Guangxi, she ranks second only to the karst mountain peaks of Guilin, those darlings, for long centuries, of poets and painters and pilgrims.

Hidden inside these mountains, inside these many incarnations, was this young woman, blessed with an angel's voice, singing all these years——inside her people's mountain songs, inside coquettish improvisations——the music of all of our hearts.

二

我有幸以诗人身份数次访游中国，曾受邀去北京参与国际写作计划，在鲁迅文学院待过一个月，也曾参加过在香港、杭州、西昌、汨罗和成都举办的诗歌节，算得上半个中国通，但不知何故，与刘三姐却总无缘相会，直到黄少政教授将她的诗歌和故事带到我眼前。对鱼峰山和广西漓江畔回荡着刘三姐山歌的群山，我一直心怀憧憬，无奈刘三姐总是从我的世界路过。1961年的电影我没看过，此前那部火遍中国大江南北、令毛主席也如痴如醉的音乐剧我也没看过，就连从2004年起就蜚声国际的绚丽多彩的户外声光秀《印象·刘三姐》，我都不知其名，对刘三姐这个壮族文化象征、桂林名片一无所知，我着实赧然。

在我未读到少政的译文，不曾结识刘三姐的时光里，她似乎已被赋予了千百次新生。她受山民景仰爱戴，被转化为精神符号，经过无数次解读、诠释、想象与塑造；她的故事也被接受、化用。而现在，我已读过了关于刘三姐的研究，看过了电影，也演奏了她的歌谣，能在黄少政教授的翻译中邂逅这位灵动善辩、胆识过人、天仙一般的壮族民谣歌者，我感到三生有幸。（我又多了一个理由让自己前往桂林游览，现在这本书就成了我的最佳导游。）

少政的译文含蓄自然，毫无浮嚣之气，我在其中遇见了纯真的刘三姐和她的歌谣。少政将刘三姐与人们以各种方式重构的形象剥离开来，返本归元，还原了她的本来面目，赋予她人性、女性特质和民族特异性，

2

It has been my good fortune to travel many times to China as a poet. I have spent a month in Beijing at the Lu Xun Academy, a guest of the international writers' program; I have attended festivals in Hong Kong, Hangzhou, Xichang, Miluo, and Chengdu. I have read widely in Chinese poetry. But somehow, until Professor Huang Shaozheng introduced me to her songs and her life, Third Sister Liu had eluded me. I have longed to visit Yufeng and the mountains her songs ring with, along the Li River, in Guangxi, but Third Sister Liu, herself, had eluded me. I had not watched the 1961 film; I had not seen the musical that preceded it, which travelled China and stole the heart of Chairman Mao; I had not, to my shame, heard of the world-famous high-tech, light-and-sound outdoor spectacular running in Guilin since 2004, *Impressions of Liu Sanjie*, which celebrates her as an emblem of Zhuang culture, a synecdoche for Guilin.

Before I met her in my friend's translations, Liu Sanjie had already lived, it seems, a thousand lives. She had been worshipped and celebrated among her people of the hills; she had been venerated and received and repurposed; she had been interpreted, reinterpreted, reimagined, and rebadged; she had been adopted and she had appropriated. Having now read the Liu Sanjie scholarship and seen the movie and played the songs, I am glad to meet her, myself, in Professor Huang Shaozheng's translations——this feisty, plucky, angelic Zhuang folk singer. (And now I have a new reason to visit Guilin, and in this book I now have the perfect guide.)

It is herself and her songs, in themselves, I feel I meet in this unpretentious translation. For Shaozheng reclaims Third Sister Liu from every way she has been borrowed and restores her to herself; he gives her back to her humanity

还读者一个赤子般的刘三姐。

我们在刘三姐歌谣中和一个不凡的灵魂不期而遇，她不附庸任何人，天生丽质，这是大山的产物，野性、不羁、爱是她的最高信仰。因而在她的歌谣里，我们与自我不期而遇——一个尚未被觉察的更好的自我，若有她一半锐气，本可以成为的那种自我。

其实我们每个人心底都有一个刘三姐，只不过我们需要聆听刘三姐的歌谣，就像我们必须阅读李白、密罗跛伊、狄金森、阿赫玛托娃，他们会引领我们省察自己的人生，返璞归真，更富于人性。别忘记，超越性别、阶层、身份（被强加的、抗拒的、认定的），拨开上天的眷顾、亏待，比坎坷、苦难和宿命更深的灵魂深处，有一片群山，群山的歌谣真切悦耳，如莺啼百啭；有一个自我，铮铮玉骨，唱着山中浩歌，遗世独立，陶然自乐而心怀悲悯。

三

少政以全新的视角解读了刘三姐，他不拘泥于此前人们建构的刘三姐形象，邀请我们一道从全新的角度走近她。此前，刘三姐是才华横溢、天真无邪的传统儒家闺秀，也是阶级革命的英雄，而少政独辟蹊径，将她与这些形象剥离。摆脱了先入之见，我们就能静候佳音，在山歌中邂逅一位歌唱家和作家，壮族人民的女神，一个凡人，但确实天赋异禀，一个有血有肉的人。

少政帮助我们欣赏到了纯真的刘三姐山歌。刘三姐曾被挪用、改编

and femininity and the specificity of her country; and he gives her back to us.

In her songs one meets a human being who belonged to no one but herself, who belonged to no cause but the mountains', and most of whose politics was love. In her songs, consequently, one meets oneself: one's unfamiliar better self; the person we would be if we had half her courage.

For inside each of us lives someone like Liu Sanjie. But we need to read her songs, as we need to read the poems of Li Bai or Mirabai or Dickinson or Akhmatova, to remember how we really go, deep down there in our humanity——to be reminded that deeper than our gender, than our class, than our identity (conferred or denied or asserted); deeper than our privilege or our disadvantage, than our trauma or our trouble or our fortune, there are mountains and their songs, sweet and true as birdsong; there is a singing self, indomitable and joyous, beautiful and kind. One of the ways that goes is how Liu Sanjie's songs go.

3

Huang Shaozheng reads Liu Sanjie freshly, and in his introduction, he invites us to read her freshly, too, unconstrained by how she's been, to date, construed. He lets her stand clear of the types she's been cast in: brilliant Confucian ingenue, and proto-revolutionary class heroine. If we can free ourselves of preconceptions, we will stand ready to meet the singer and a writer, the woman of her people, any one of us at all (though more gifted), this flesh-and-blood human, who turns up in these songs.

I've said Professor Shaozheng helps us see Liu Sanjie's work in itself, that

以服务于各种目的：古代家长制对她形象的塑造、20世纪60年代社会现实主义对她的新解读。少政别出心裁，他提出了两种审视刘三姐山歌的路径，并在翻译中遵循了这两种路径。

首先，少政明智地建议我们把刘三姐山歌视作特定地理位置与当地盛行的文化规范的实体（这些文化规范在固守传统的地方依然盛行）。在聆听这些歌谣时，多多少少把它看作是一种特定时代民俗的结果。所有艺术作品中都包含情爱的因素，在我看来不无道理，因为艺术是参与创作的行为，一种爱的行为，一种渴望的抒发，一种对美的欢颂，一种狂喜瞬间的定格（亦可以是希冀与绝望）。然而许多文学理论研究，尤其是那些透过权力和经济的关系、阶级、社会类别、既定道德以及各种规范性抽象视角的解读，似乎并不能阐明诗与歌的灵感源泉。诗歌可以来源于忧痛、激愤、欢悦与怡乐；诗歌有所希冀乃至心灰意冷；写诗是对生活不如意与世界不堪的补偿，或对生命本身的感恩，和生活本质的凡俗庸常达成坦然的和解。

奥克塔维奥·帕斯写道，"诗歌即是语言做爱"，这就比西方流行的许多文学论调更切题。正如我最近一篇文章里写的："无论爱为何物，诗即爱。"如果读懂了刘三姐的歌谣，我们不妨说，确实有一种大爱，叫作山歌。刘三姐的诗歌是爱与欲，温软如玉的呢喃，有慈悲有希望，也有惶惑有尖刺，更有对所爱之人与世人所爱的渴求，也是对积存在世壮族山歌的升华。山歌本就是壮族歌圩的核心，传唱山歌在于和心爱之人共情，而非一定要落实在婚姻之中，心心相印才是这一活动的必要条件。壮族文化历来重视恋爱自由，当代读者也会惊讶于他们的开明。

he stands her clear of how she has been stolen from herself by the uses to which she has been put——the paternalistic pre-modern construction, and the social realist reinterpretation of the 1960s. But Huang Shaozheng reads her, too. He proposes two ways of seeing her in herself. And he translates her with those inflections in mind.

Very sensibly, for starters, Huang Shaozheng suggests that we consider Liu Sanjie's oeuvre as a manifestation of its place and of the cultural norms that prevailed there (and prevail still where traditional practices thrive). I would have thought it made sense to consider the role of the erotic in all works of art——since art is a participation in creation, an act, generally, of love, an articulation of longing, a celebration of beauty, a moment of ecstasy (of hope or despair etc). But many theoretical readings of literature——in particular those that see through prisms of power and economic relations, of class, of social category, of settled moralities, of various normative abstractions—— seem innocent of the wellsprings of poetry and song. One writes from grief and anger and joy and delight; one writes in hope or despair; one writes to run lyric repairs on one's life and all lives; one writes out of gratitude for being alive among all that is beautiful and all that is not.

When Octavio Paz writes that "poetry is language making love," he is more on the money than many theoretical readings that prevail in the west. As I say in a recent essay, "whatever love is, poetry does that." If all literature might be better understood, then, as the practice of affection, seduction, tender recollection, compassion, hope, dismay, provocation, or yearning (for a human beloved or for the beloved in the world), this is even more manifestly the case for Liu Sanjie's songs, which honoured and transfigured established Zhuang mountain songs, which were themselves a central part of the courting rituals

无论爱为何物，诗即爱：正统文学理论向来难以理解接受这一概念，可事实如此，以诗性的行为和壮族的歌圩文化来理解刘三姐山歌，聆听歌中人性的淳朴，而非将其看作意识形态的实例或仅仅是体现政治和身份的形式，如此一来，恍然间，歌声里的那些拨云撩雨、嬉笑斯磨、暧昧难明、感官愉悦与玩世不恭，霎时一一入耳，了然于心。

少政的另一大突破是将刘三姐的山歌解读为群山的造化，提供了生态批评的解读思路。所谓山歌，与野性、不羁、天真未凿、未经文明浸染同化同义。

这就是说，少政引导我们不要单纯地将刘三姐的山歌上升为民族家国的呼声，钩沉阶级斗争乃至民族身份的因由，抑或只探究其文学作品的底色，这些山歌更像是描摹了中国南方的万千气象、岩溶起伏，是对湍流急雨和莽莽榛榛山地的鲜活注解。壮族文化，包括其中的情爱因素，都是由山地孕育而生的，所谓地理即宿命。在刘三姐的歌谣里，你能找到一个女性生存的土地与根基，蓦然回首，忆起你亦寄身在这世上的某一处所，而在你的生命中、你的文字间、你的情感深处，分明也有大地的旋律涌动。也许这世上某个角落还记得你，于是你的笔触、你的声音、你的双手和生命都在娓娓道来，诉说它的故事，它的今生和来世。

of the Zhuang people, songs which were made and shared to help one make amatory progress——to score, not necessarily a husband or wife, but certainly a lover. For Zhuang culture has always valued freedom of love, in particular before marriage, in a way that contemporary readers might find surprisingly broad-minded.

Whatever love is, poetry does that: a concept theory has always struggled to understand or accept. But so it is, it seems, with Liu Sanjie's songs, and invited to hear her words in their humanity, as practices of poetry, of Zhuang courting rites, not as instances of ideology or merely as enactments of politics and identity, one suddenly hears the flirtation, feels the playfulness, discerns the innuendo, enjoys the sensuality, understands more fully the irreverence, in these songs.

A second and equally sensible innovation in Huang Shaozheng's reading of Liu Sanjie is his invitation to see them as manifestations of the mountains in which they came into being. He offers an ecocritical reading. These are mountain songs, and if one feels allowed, on can hear the mountains in them.

Shaozheng invites us, then, to consider in the songs and life of Liu Sanjie as expressions not just national aspiration, nor of class struggle, nor even merely of ethnic identity, nor yet merely as literary artefacts, but as expressions of the weather in China's south, of the steepness of the karst slopes, and the swiftness of the rivers and the hardness of the rain and the difficulty of the soil. Zhuang culture, including its erotic charge, is what it is because of where it evolved. Geography is destiny, as it has been said. In these songs, then, find the ground of one woman's being, and recall that you, too, are home somewhere on this earth, and in your life and in your word and in how you love, geography sings; there is perhaps a place that remembers you, and in the work or your

四

国家与事业、反叛与治国，理论家与卫道士，世间形形色色的势力无不试图"征用"艺术。他们扶植艺术宣传自己的主张，发掘既往的作品，彰显同质价值观，或因其缺乏此类价值观而痛陈其堕落退化。

然而，真正的艺术本质上不会屈从、附庸任何权势。大浪淘沙，披沙拣金，艺术永恒。世人攘攘，政治浮沉，艺术如青山依旧，几度夕阳。极而言之，人类少不了艺术，人性健全有赖于艺术。作家、歌手、画家正可以大显身手。存在的喜悦和悲苦，日复一日世间的粗粝与敏感灵魂的二律背反，生活的美好与可怖，艺术就是见证。人生苦短，艺术必须为我们安身立命提供一个说法。悲苦不堪的世间，爱是如何可能？希望与妄想有何分际？我们需要艺术发声，我们指望艺术作证。艺术源于人生，高于人生。人类多数的理论话语往往会忽略深植于人性的这种渴求，不单单忽略，更有甚者，贬低、污名化人性的需求，艺术的出场，为人性正名，为悲悯张目，并在我们的心灵惶惶然处发现了极美的趣致。

艺术的目的，正如我在中国西昌一篇演讲中宣示的，就是自由，就

voice or hands or life, you manifest something of what that place knows and how it goes.

4

States and causes, rebels and rulers, theorists and defenders of prevailing intellectual norms——all these forces, everywhere on earth, want to recruit art. They sponsor new work that practises ideals they value; and they find in old work manifestations of those same values, or evidence of degeneracy in the absence of those values.

But real art is not for bending; it endures and survives. Beyond the shifting causes and beliefs and theories that seek to recruit art, art is needed. Humanity needs it. And writers and singers and painters will always supply that need. Which is to bear witness to the pain and delight, the infernal contradiction, the beauty and the terror entailed in Being: What it feels like to live a short while on an astonishing and sometimes appalling Earth, how one goes about fashioning meaning from the chaos of things, how one hopes and loves, notwithstanding the evidence to hand. This is why we need art, and it is what art has always tried (even without knowing it) to articulate. And we need art to keep doing that because it alone does justice to the felt-sense of being alive. Whereas most other discourses overlook our humanity, diminish it or disdain it, art (songs such as these) sees us. Art allows us and redeems us in our ordinary humanity. Art alone forgives us for being human. It makes beauty of our confusion.

Art, then, as I found myself saying in a paper I gave once in Xichang, is

是正义。艺术凭其新奇巧思和清正之气，助我们跳出陈腐与伪善的樊笼，挣脱主流正统的桎梏，表达自由和富于个性的声音，传递艺术家的生活体验。几许匠心，赋予了人生真实的触感，谱写了心灵专属的乐律。

在少政的刘三姐歌谣新译中，自由、喜悦、正义，声声入耳，我们与大地脉动同频共振——世界以爱予我，我亦报之以情。刘三姐的歌是唱给群山的情歌，是对大千世界爱的倾诉。

上周日我听一个学生说起，诗人就要腹有诗书，兰心蕙质。她说起她的先生，一位诗人，相濡以沫经年。她说起历史上那些著名的大诗人。她说，诗人需要从生活和书本中汲取各种养分，包括思想、历史、音乐、韵律、品格、人性，甚至熟稔植物与禽鸟的学名。果如此，他必须真正走出书斋，学贯百家，臻于会通，才能出口成章，作诗撰文。一个诗人的资质尚且如此，一个译者又要如何万里行路，万卷读书呢？

翻译的确需要一种虚怀若谷的大智慧、豁达冲淡的心境、挥毫落纸的劲头，并守住一份情怀。用母语自然能够畅言真实的所感所念，但若假自己之口，移译他人言语又是另一码事。盖因每种语言自成一世界，译者功夫再深都难以彻悟并在另一种语言中再造原作者的声音、思想和笔调——任何译作都是一部新作。即便译文能传神达意，在形式、情感、态度、音韵、文气和寓意上固然都能忠实于原作，但译作永远不会取代原作。

for freedom and it is for justice. In its freshness and originality and integrity, it frees us from cliché and cant; in its freedom from orthodoxy, in its individuality of voice, it does justice to an artist's lived experience, and it justifies, in its own sui-generis achievement, the authenticity of each human life; it justifies and allows the particular music of each human heart.

One hears all this——the freedom, the joy, the justice——in Huang Shaozheng's new translations of the songs of Liu Sanjie. One hears the heartbeat of the Earth——how the Earth loves us and how it would be loved in return. These folk songs are a kind of love song to the mountains, and beyond them all the Earth.

Poets have to know so much, I heard a student say last Sunday. She had in mind a poet whom she'd been married to for many years; she had in mind the many she had read. And she meant how much the poet has to study in life and in books about ideas and history and speech music and metrics and characters and about human nature and the names of trees and birds. It's true you have to get out a bit and go to many different kinds of school and get across disparate bodies of knowledge to make poetry and other forms of literature. But how much more then must the translator know.

Truly, translation is a practice of deep humility and great wisdom, of generosity and courage and faith. It is one thing to sit in one's own language and say what one perceives to be real and to matter; it is another to take the authentic utterance of another and to seek to do justice to it in one's own voice in a tongue the first speaker could not speak. Because each language is another universe, and because the translator, no matter how hard she tries, will not divine and recast in a new tongue the voice and mind and manner of the author of the original work, in her mother tongue——each translation is new work. If

质量上乘的译品，其意境与原作基本相当，能够再现原作的精神，且在形式上尽可能地效仿原作。作为一种介质、替代品和备选方案，它在功能上等同于原作。这桩活计谁人能够胜任？好坏读者自有公论——拙见非我的朋友少政莫属。除了译者本人，还会有谁能如此钟情于原作，并绞尽脑汁将其原汁原味呈现给读者呢？正是像少政这样的翻译家，他们大大地丰富了我们的世界。我把他们的工作，视为爱的奉献。我无时无刻不对他们心怀感激。我之所以能同托尔斯泰，能同诗人鲁米、阿赫玛托娃、萨福、吉狄马加、屈原、李清照、《圣经·旧约·雅歌》莫逆于心，正是拜翻译所赐。也正是李牧原最早的译本、黄少政等对我的译介，将我的作品带到了中国，用汉语赋予了我的诗文第二次生命。

　　笔者不谙中文，无法在这里对译文质量做出专业判断。但我知道少政是一位优秀的译者。例如，他将《新约》和纪伯伦的诗歌翻译成中文，将吉狄马加的诗歌和演讲翻译成英语。他被视为当下中国最杰出的双语翻译家之一。少政博学并极富灵性，酷爱世界文学。他如此醉心译介刘三姐歌谣，部分原因是他定居广西，而广西正是刘三姐歌谣的故乡。我还知道他比对研究了之前刘三姐歌谣的其他译本，新的译文大异于从前，他试图在英语中捕捉到早期译本中缺失的某些特殊品质——质朴、感性、戏谑和柔情，早期的译文不可避免囿于彼时翻译习惯和流行教条的影响。

it is honourably performed and well-achieved, it will, of course, be faithful in form and mood and attitude and voice and sense and implication to the original. But it can never be that original work.

A good translation gives a close impression. It adequates the original; it approximates it. It stands in for it, a proxy, a substitute, an alternate. And who would perform this work, which inevitably invites comparison and critique, but someone passionately dedicated to the work they translate? Who but a dedicatee, a lover of the original work would labour to bring to a new readership a faithful likeness? The world is immeasurably richer because of the work of translators, and I think of their work, including that of my friend Huang, as the work of love. I express my gratitude to them every day. I would have no Tolstoy, no Rumi, no Akhmatova, no Sappho, no Jidi Majia, no Qu Yuan, no Li Qingzhao, no *Song of Songs*, without translators. And my work would not have come to China without Isabelle Li, who translated it first, or without Huang and others, who have given my poems and essays a second life in Chinese.

I don't know Chinese well enough to make that judgment here. But I know that Professor Shaozheng is a fine translator. He has translated, for instance, the *New Testament* and the poetry of Kahil Gibran into Chinese, and the poetry and speeches of Jidi Majia into English. I know he is respected as one of China's most accomplished translators, and I know him to be a man of spirituality and a profound love for world literature. I know that he loves the songs he is translating, in part because he is a native of Guangxi, the region of China sung by Liu Sanjie. And I know that he has studied other translations of Liu and followed them here and departed from them there, in order to catch in English the particular qualities——the earthiness, the sensuality, the play,

少政还发愿要让刘三姐在英语中唱响。要像在汉语中那样唱得惊天地泣鬼神，绝非译者的本意，但至少要让英语读者听众感受到刘三姐的歌谣有多么优美动听，这一点也不算奢求。

摆在你面前的这部刘三姐歌谣新译，译者试图剥离不同时代的意识形态的"征用"与道德的"挪用"，还原刘三姐歌谣的产生背景和发生场域，重新审视刘三姐传说故事的结构性因素——源于壮族的歌圩文化，带领我们穿越时空，亲耳聆听唱响在旖旎喀斯特山水间的天籁——刘三姐歌谣。透过黄少政的这部译作，我们读到了一个鲜活生动、漂亮机敏、大胆奔放、为民请命的乡野女性，足堪我们追慕一种自由本真的性灵，师法一种朴素高贵的人生。

（焦琳 译）

and the tenderness——missing in earlier translations, inflected as they were by older and more formal mores and dogmas.

The hope of the translator is that their translation seem a good song in the host language. Not as good as the original was in its mother tongue——that would be a fool's ambition. But a good enough song, striking and original in the same sort of way that the original was.

Here, then, is Liu Sanjie, freed from others' orthodoxies, walking in the integrity of her own ideas, in the music of her own heart, in the weather of her own culture, in the idiom of her own mountain realm. Liberated by this humane rendering of her profoundly human life and works, in which each of us can find a self it's still not too late yet to be, a life it's not too late to live.

第一部分　歌舞剧《刘三姐》剧本

Part One　Full Text of the Script of the Musical Drama

第一部分内容为歌舞剧《刘三姐》(1961年版)全剧剧本翻译。该剧本根据邓昌伶同名剧本改编，编剧为曾昭文、龚邦榕、邓凡平、牛秀、黄勇刹、包玉堂。

This text was collectively written by Zeng Zhaowen, Gong Bangrong, Deng Fanping, Niu Xiu, Huang Yongcha and Bao Yutang, published in 1961, based on the namesake opera by Deng Changling.

人物

刘三姐　刘　二　老渔翁

莫　福　小　牛　二猎手

莫进财　众家丁　韦老奶

兰　芬　冬　妹　春　姐

众姑娘　亚　木　亚　祥

众青年　莫海仁　四丫鬟

王媒婆　陶秀才　李秀才

罗秀才　众歌伴　外乡人

Characters

Third Sister　Liu'er　Old Fisherman

Mo Fu　Xiaoniu　Two Hunters

Steward Mo　Servants　Grandma Wei

Lanfen　Dongmei　Chunjie

Girls　Yamu　Yaxiang

Young Men　Lord Mo　Four Maids

Matchmaker Wang　Scholar Tao　Scholar Li

Scholar Luo　Singers　Strangers

第一场　投亲

时　　古代。

景　　山峰蜿蜒重叠，江流曲曲弯弯，一片红色的早霞，映现在山峦的隐处。

　　　春风拂面，清晰、舒畅。顺着流水，飘来了刘三姐的歌声。

三　姐　（内唱）

　　　　唱山歌，

　　　　这边唱来那边和，

　　　　山歌好比春江水，

　　　　不怕滩险弯又多。

　　　　歌声中，须眉皓白的老渔翁，驾着一只小船，载着三姐、刘二上。

三　姐　（唱）

　　　　唱歌好，

　　　　树木招手鸟来和，

　　　　江心鲤鱼跳出水，

　　　　要和三姐对山歌。

老渔翁　小姑娘，你唱得好，唱得好，把我这七十岁的老头迷住了。

刘　二　老伯，你莫夸奖我妹子了。

ACT ONE
The Fruits Do Not Tumble Far from the Tree

Time: Long, long time ago.

Venue: A magnificent country where a river is meandering through hills and a new day dawns in the valley.

(The winter's reign has come to an end. Bright skies and agreeable warmth, chirping of birds, the sweet odors of spring on the breeze. Third Sister's singing echoes along the stream.)

Third Sister (*delirious with joy*):

Follow me all the way,

On both river banks we are singing along,

Like river waters my songs flow,

Cutting across shoals and skirting bends.

(During this song enter the old fisherman, white-brewed and bearded, who is kind to row her and her brother to seek their ancestral village and kinsmen.)

Third Sister (*thrilling at the prospect of nearing her native place*):

Singing is my passion,

Trees swing and birds come to me;

Carp leap out the middle of the river,

All to try out my musical talent.

Old Fisherman: What a voice! Lass, indeed, matchless singing! You have bewitched an old man of seventy.

Liu'er: Don't flatter my sister, uncle.

三　姐　（唱）

　　　　莫夸我，

　　　　画眉取笑小阳雀，

　　　　黄嘴嫩鸟才学唱，

　　　　绒毛鸭仔初下河。

刘　二　三妹，你不要唱了好不好？

三　姐　老伯，你来唱，我来学。

老渔翁　要我唱？哈！

　　　　哈……（唱）

　　　　要我唱，

　　　　牙齿不全口漏风，

　　　　我若开口唱一句，

　　　　虾公鱼仔脸都红。

　　　　这时红日已升上江面，照得通红。

三　姐　（唱）

　　　　老伯莫讲口漏风，

　　　　唱得云开日头红，

　　　　山歌好比拦江网，

　　　　鱼鳖虾蟹落网中。

刘　二　下滩了！

老渔翁　下滩了！

　　　　一流急水，小船摇荡地冲了过去，刘二为之一震。

刘　二　三妹，水急浪高，你要站稳了！

三　姐　（唱）

Third Sister (*blushing*):

> You have been pulling my legs,
>
> I have learned much from you all.
>
> A baby lark for a while babbling away,
>
> A chick duck hitting the water just now.

Liu'er: Can't you behave like a woman, sister?

Third Sister: Uncle, come on. You still can sing from experience and I won't lose this opportunity to learn from you.

Old Fisherman: I am afraid I will make a poor show of myself instead. Oho...

> (*jestingly*)
>
> Are you sure I must stand to be counted,
>
> Now my teeth half gone, my senile voice grading into gruffness.
>
> Should a note come out of my mouth,
>
> I fear prawn and fish might blush for me.

> (*The sun has risen and shone brightly across the stream.*)

Third Sister (*awed by such sonorous voice*):

> Modesty compels you to say so;
>
> You do have right to sing from experience,
>
> To dissipate the clouds before ushering in the glowing sun.
>
> A net laid across the river garnering the largest crop of fish.

Liu'er: Uncle, we've come to the rapids!

Old Fisherman: Yes, the rapids!

> (*The boat picks speed and rocks in the swift current. Liu'er barely loses balance.*)

Liu'er: The current is rough, sister. Don't lose your balance.

Third Sister (*exuberantly*):

浪滔滔，

河里鱼虾都来朝，

急水滩头唱一句，

风平浪静乐逍遥。

刘　二　三妹，风也没有平，浪也没有静，你怎么就不懂得怕？

三　姐　（唱）

浪送船行风送帆，

唱起山歌湾过湾，

山歌唱破千层浪，

闯过一滩又一滩。

老渔翁　唱得好……

又是一流急水，小船又被冲到另一边。

老渔翁　（镇静地，唱）

过了一滩又一滩，

莫怕艰险莫怕难，（一时唱不出口。）

三　姐　（接唱）

只要留得长流水，

有朝冲倒九重山。

老渔翁　（有所领悟地重复这两句，唱）

只要留得长流水，

有朝冲倒九重山。

小姑娘，你唱得太好了！你是哪里人！高姓呵？

Waves tumble and swirl,

Yet fish and prawns bob up to salute;

One tune out of my mouth at the rapids,

Lo! The wind calms down and the waves rest.

Liu'er: This is really rough, sister. Aren't you ever afraid?

Third Sister (*in a mood of exhilaration*):

Rapid after rapid, and rounds of shoals and bends skirted,

We go at them undaunted and unafraid.

So long as tide is at a high picking up a momentum,

It will roar all the way into the sea.

Old Fisherman: Encore!

(*The boat is swept to one side in another rapid, but the old fisherman keeps presence of mind.*)

Old Fisherman (*inspired*):

From rapid to rapid, shoal to shoal,

We have rowed all the way.

(*The old fishman is at a loss to go on, but Third Sister continues.*)

Third Sister (*euphorically*):

So long as the rivers roll on,

Wherever we want to go ashore.

(*The old fisherman, sensing her meaning, repeats.*)

Old Fisherman (*euphorically*):

Yes, so long as the rivers roll on,

Wherever we want to go ashore.

You're a very good singer, lass! Where are you from? What's your name?

刘 二　三妹，不要讲了。老伯，靠岸吧！

老渔翁　好，好，靠岸了。

　　　　兄妹正上岸，幕内有争吵声，莫家的家丁莫福手提野兔，大摇大摆地走上。一彪壮的青年——小牛，和两个青年猎手随后赶来。

小 牛　放下！
莫 福　老子拿你一只野兔来下酒，是赏你的脸。

小 牛　你好无理！
莫 福　穷鬼，睁开眼睛看看大爷是哪家的！（举拳就打。）

小 牛　我认识你是莫家的一条狗！（从莫福手里夺回猎物，并将他一脚踢倒。）
莫 福　你还打人，哼，我禀报我家老爷，你休想再在这里打猎！

小 牛　你仗着莫家势力为非作歹……

　　　　莫进财与二家丁从一边上。

莫进财　什么事？
莫 福　莫管家，我好说好讲和他要一只野兔给老爷下酒，这穷鬼不识抬举，张口就骂……

莫进财　好大的胆子，来呀！把猎物取下！

Liu'er: Please, sister, could you be a bit more reticent about? Uncle, will you put us ashore?

Old Fisherman: All right, I will moor here for you to debark.

(*As they are reaching ashore, angry cries are heard offstage. Mo Fu, an underling of local tyrant, Lord Mo, swaggers in with a hare in his hand. A young man Xiaoniu pursues him with two other young hunters.*)

Xiaoniu: Return us our game!

Mo Fu (*brazenly*)**:** Your game comes in handy. I will sort of feast with wine and I'm doing you an honor.

Xiaoniu (*snapping*)**:** Shame on you. It is our hunt.

Mo Fu (*haughtily*)**:** You are getting far too cheeky! Open your eyes, creature! What family do I serve, you know? (*He raises his fist to strike.*)

Xiaoniu (*scornfully*)**:** Everybody knows you're a petty minion of the Mo family. (*He snatches the hare from Mo Fu and kicks him over.*)

Mo Fu (*smarting for his impudence*)**:** You dare raise a hand against me! My master shall look into this case and you'll never be able to hunt here again.

Xiaoniu (*earning himself a scolding*)**:** You bloody crook! You're nothing but a nuisance to the villagers. All you do is to play the bully, attack people and suck up to the powerful. How could you be horrible? (*Enter the steward with two servants.*)

Steward: What's the row?

Mo Fu (bowing and scraping)**:** I have been kind enough to, so to speak, sir, to ask him to let me his newly hunted hare for our master to feast with wine. But this wretched moron declines to forgo his small animal——he even starts using four letter words at me...

Steward (*glaring at Xiaoniu*)**:** That is too much! Here, this flagrant wrong must be

家丁欲上，几个青年怒目而视，家丁犹疑，不敢力夺。

三　姐　（唱）

　　　　天地山川盘古开，

　　　　飞禽走兽众人财，

　　　　想吃鲜鱼就撒网，

　　　　要吃野兔带箭来。

莫进财　你是什么人？可晓得莫家的厉害！

三　姐　（唱）

　　　　大路不平众人踩，

　　　　情理不合众人抬；

　　　　横梁不正刀斧砍，

　　　　管你是斜还是歪！

莫进财　你……你……

　　　　刘二阻止三姐。

老渔翁　喂！莫大管家，他们是外乡人，不晓得你莫家的厉害。算了吧，为了一只野兔争吵不休，叫外人看来也有失你莫家的体面。哈哈哈！

　　　　众人大笑。

莫进财　哼！你们这些刁蛮，不愿和你们生这些闲气。走！（下。）

readdressed!

(*The servants turn to Xiaoniu for the bone of contention, but the young hunters advance on them so that they dare not nab it back.*)

Third Sister (*rebuffing Lord Mo's lackeys*):

Heaven and earth deities conferred upon us.

Pheasants and animals are all men's prey.

To lunch on fish, just cast out your net;

To dine on hares, bring your arrows along.

Steward (*startled*): Who are you? Don't you know my lord is making his rules and running the show in the neighborhood?

Third Sister (*ignoring his threat, proclaiming*):

When a road is rough, we tread it flat.

When an argument makes little sense, we beg to differ.

It takes an axe to straighten out a crooked beam;

Chopping or hacking, it all depends.

Steward (*falteringly*): you...

(*Liu'er hushes Third Sister down.*)

Old Fisherman (*interrupting to smooth thing out*): Ah, steward, they are but strangers newly landed in our village. They have yet to figure out who is who in the community. Don't bother about what they say. But to me, a steward like you makes such a fuss about a small animal, I am afraid, you suffer the Mo family lose face in front of outsiders. Ha, ha, ha!

(*The others laugh.*)

Steward (*obviously glad of the interruption*): Bah! It is not worth messing around with bumpkins like you. Let's go. (*Exit.*)

莫福、家丁随下。

老渔翁 真是个又聪明又胆大的小姑娘!

小　牛 (走向老渔翁,惊奇又胆怯地问)这位姐姐是哪里来的?

刘　二 莫夸奖我妹子了,她就是爱唱歌惹是生非!

老渔翁 你妹子唱歌人人爱听,好似热茶暖透心。

刘　二 唉!老伯,你不晓得呀! (唱)

　　　　我兄妹,在罗城,

　　　　砍柴织笠度光阴,

　　　　三妹年幼性执拗,

　　　　不知天高和海深,

　　　　皆因唱歌惹……惹了事,

　　　　这才离乡弃土来投亲。

老渔翁 来投亲? (看着三姐,又看刘二)你们是不是来找韦老奶的?

小　牛 找韦老奶的!

三姐、刘二 老伯,你怎么晓得?

老渔翁 同条村子共条河,哪家的亲戚老汉我不晓得?你是韦老奶的外孙女,爱唱山歌的刘三姐。

小　牛 哦!刘三姐!

　　　　小牛示意二青年猎手去告诉韦老奶,二青年猎手下。

(*Exit with Mo Fu and the other servants.*)

Old Fisherman: This girl has some guts. Hurrah!

Xiaoniu (*awed by her gallantry*)**:** What wind has blown this brave girl here?

Liu'er: Don't talk so patronizingly. Singing is her weakness that always lands us in trouble.

Old Fisherman: Your sister's songs prove so irresistible. They're so much heartwarming like a cup of tea.

Liu'er: Ah, uncle, I am afraid you don't know what kind of mess we are caught in. (*apologetically*)

We have come from afar,

Where we make a living by cutting wood and plaiting straw hats;

But my young sister, with so much veracity,

Has no sense of dangers in life at all.

Her pert singing is in particular troublesome,

Till we have to flee to seek refuge and look for kinsmen here.

Old Fisherman: To look for kinsmen, eh? (*He stares at Third Sister, then at Liu'er.*) You must be locating an old lady called Grandma Wei?

Xiaoniu: Grandma Wei?

Third Sister and Liu'er: How did you know, uncle?

Old Fisherman (*beaming with satisfaction*)**:** It so happens we all live in the same village by the same river, of course I know what kith and kin each family has. You are Grandma Wei's grand-daughter Third Sister, and a musical wizard, so to speak.

Xiaoniu: Third Sister!

(*He gesticulates to the two other hunters to notify Grandma Wei. They go out.*)

三　姐　老伯，你怎么猜到的？

老渔翁　（念）

　　　　高山打鼓远闻声，

　　　　三姐唱歌久闻名，

　　　　二十七钱摆三注，

　　　　九文九文又九文。（"九文"同"久闻"音。）

三　姐　老伯，你讲笑话了。

　　　　韦老奶、兰芬、冬妹、春姐等上。

韦老奶　呵！我的外孙女，你长得这样高大了！

刘二、三姐　外婆！

兰　芬　三表姐！

三　姐　你是兰芬表妹！

小　牛　我叫李小牛。三姐，你人我没见过，你的歌我们早就会唱了。

众　人　（唱）

　　　　山歌一唱起春风，

　　　　穷人一唱乐融融，

　　　　唱得一禾生九穗，

　　　　唱得黑夜太阳红。

　　　　——幕徐落

Third Sister: It is very kind of you to say so! Uncle !

Old Fisherman (*respectfully*):

      Drums are sounding on the hilltop,

      To harbinger the landing of a real glory on our shores.

      She is such a legend, the pride of our nation,

      That her presence is hotly sought.

Third Sister: You are joking with me, uncle!

      (*Enter Grandma Wei, Lanfen, Dongmei and Chunjie.*)

Grandma Wei: Ah, my grand-daughter has grown up!

Liu'er and Third Sister: Granny!

Lanfen: Cousin!

Third Sister: Are you cousin Lanfen?

Xiaoniu: I am Xiaoniu of the Li family. We've never met, Third Sister, but we

      have heard much talk of you and your unusual musical talent.

Together (*soothingly*):

      Singing affords us a relief from daily grinding,

      Alleviating much of our concern;

      We'll sing of better revenue for our blood and sweat,

      We sing till things turn around in our favor.

      (*Curtain.*)

第二场　霸山

时　　一年后。

景　　春天的山野，满山满坡都是青翠的茶树，万绿丛中夹杂着火红的
　　　　杜鹃花。

　　　　兰芬和几个姑娘手提茶篮边唱边舞上。

众姑娘　（唱）

　　　　春天茶叶嫩又鲜，

　　　　姐妹双双走茶园；

　　　　满山茶树妹手种，

　　　　辛勤换得茶满园。

　　　　春天茶叶香又香，

　　　　茶山一片好风光；

　　　　自己种来自己采，

　　　　甜满心头香满筐。

兰　芬　姐妹们，你们看哪！这茶枝密密的，茶叶多多的，……

老渔翁　（暗上）味道香香的。

众姑娘　老公公来啦。

兰　芬　老公公，看我们这茶山好不好？

老渔翁　前几年是一片荒山野岭，如今变成花果山了。

　　　　（唱）

　　　　满山茶树满山花，

　　　　蝴蝶采花妹采茶；

ACT TWO
Lord Mo Schemes to Plunder the Tea Plantations

Time: A year later.

Venue: Hills grown with lush tea plantations.

(*Enter Lanfen and other girls with baskets, singing and dancing.*)

Girls (*blithely*):

Maids are taking in the crop.

Tending and pruning these delicate plants with utmost care,

They have a reason to reap the harvest they deserve.

Spring turns around, with aroma permeating the plantations,

A visual sensation and a true sensual feast.

Maids reap what they plant and prune;

What more do they desire but going home with full baskets of tea leaves?

Lanfen: Look how thick the branches are, sisters, and how richly grown with tender leaves to be plucked.

(*Enters the old fisherman imperceptibly.*)

Old Fisherman: And what a sweet smell!

Girls: Why, look who's here today.

Lanfen: What do you think of our tea plantations, grandpa?

Old Fisherman: A few years ago it was a barren hill; now it's completely transformed into a treasure trove. (*rejoicing*)

Shrubs and plants overgrow the hill,

The butterflies flit to the flowers while girls pick tea;

一片茶叶香百里，

赛过园中茉莉花。

春　姐　老公公，你不在河里打鱼，来西山上做什么？

老渔翁　你们茶山的香味，姑娘们的歌声，把老汉引上来的呀！

冬　妹　老公公，自从你把三姐接来这一年多，我们学了好多歌。

兰　芬　老公公，我晓得你是来找三姐的。三姐上山打柴去了，一会儿
　　　　就回来。

老渔翁　好啦，你们快采茶吧！

兰　芬　姐妹们，采起茶来！

众姑娘　（唱）

姐妹生得灵巧手，

采茶好比绣金球；

上采好似蝶恋花，

下采好似金鱼游；

左采好似龙戏水，

右采好似凤点头；

采得春风笑开口，

采得青山笑点头。

老渔翁　（接唱）

今年采茶手提篮，

明年采茶用肩担；

长街换得红绒线，

绣个金球和哥连。

The scent of tea plantations spreads far and wide,

Sweeter than jasmine in the garden.

Chunjie: Why have you come to the western hill, grandpa, instead of fishing on the river?

Old Fisherman: What with the fragrant tea and your picking tea songs, totally enchanted, I couldn't keep away.

Dongmei: Thanks to your accommodating Third Sister, uncle, we've learned a good many songs from our famed songbird.

Lanfen: I know you're looking for Third Sister, grandpa. She's out there somewhere cutting firewood. She'll emerge anyway.

Old Fisherman: All right, go on picking your tea.

Lanfen: Let's get back to work, girls.

Girls (*blithely*):

Our nimble fingers,

Pluck tea leaves as if embroidering silk balls for our loves;

So adroitly like butterflies flitting from bud to bud,

Like goldfish swimming in the pond;

Like dragons frolicking in the water,

Or phoenixes tending their wings.

We pick till the spring breeze smiles upon us,

We pick till the green hills dance with joy.

Old Fisherman (*continuing their song in jest*):

This year you gather tea leaves in baskets,

Next year you will pick whole crates,

Barter them at the fair for crimson thread,

And embroider golden balls to toss to your lovers.

众姑娘 老公公，你又讲笑话了。

老渔翁 莫吵，你们听。

　　　　　远处传来三姐的歌声。

三　姐 （内唱）

　　　　　姐砍柴，

　　　　　挑起木柴把口开，

　　　　　木柴压弯竹扁担，

　　　　　山歌伴姐飞回来。

　　　　　亚木、亚祥和几个砍柴的小伙子上。

亚　木 趁着大家歇息，和三姐盘歌好不好？

兰　芬 人家三姐开口是歌，见什么唱什么，你哪里是她的对手。

亚　祥 怕什么，我们人多智广，又有老公公当军师，今天我们一定要
　　　　　对赢三姐。

亚　木 三姐来了。

　　　　　三姐肩挑柴担，口唱山歌上，刘二挑柴随上。

三　姐 （唱）

　　　　　阿哥阿妹上山坡，

　　　　　打得柴多歌更多，

　　　　　砍柴要砍黄连树，

　　　　　唱歌要唱欢乐歌。

　　　　　姑娘们及小伙子们拥上。

众　人 三姐！

兰　芬 三姐，你看谁来啦！

Girls: You are such a teaser, grandpa!

Old Fisherman: Hush! Listen!

(*Third Sister is heard singing in the distance.*)

Third Sister (*to herself*):

You pluck your tea leaves while I cut my firewood;

I keep singing at work, boost to both yield and morale.

Targeting bitter-wort for its heating value,

I have a large repertoire praising the good in life.

(*Enter Yamu, Yaxiang and other woodcutters.*)

Yamu: This is a break time. How about a singing duel with Third Sister?

Lanfen: Third Sister is such a virtuoso. She improvises on any theme given. She has a ready tongue for everything. How can we compete with her?

Yaxiang: Never mind. There's strength in numbers. Besides, grandpa is here to advise us. Today we stand a better chance of beating her, don't we?

Yamu: Here comes Third Sister!

(*Enter Third Sister shouldering firewood, singing, followed by Liu'er with another load of wood.*)

Third Sister (*musing*):

Brother and sister are out there up the hills,

We've cut firewood while singing;

For firewood we cut bitter-wort,

But to cheer up, we sing of happy, not sad.

(*The girls and young men rush towards her.*)

All: Third Sister!

Lanfen: Third Sister, see who's here!

刘二、三姐　老伯，好久没有见你了。

老渔翁　水上漂了一个多月，刚一靠岸，就听见你们山歌唱得热闹，两
　　　　条腿就随着耳朵走来了。

亚　祥　三姐，大家都等着和你盘歌呢。

刘　二　三妹，我先回家啦。

老渔翁　老二，你也来和大家一起唱嘛。

刘　二　不啦，我先把柴送回去。三妹，（把三姐拉到一旁，念）
　　　　唱歌莫唱是非事，
　　　　免得开口得罪人。

三　姐　二哥，你讲话才怪呢！无是无非我惹什么祸。
　　　　刘二下。

兰　芬　二哥的胆子真是和芝麻一样。

众　人　三姐，快唱呀！

亚　木　（唱）
　　　　引姐唱，
　　　　清潭起浪引鱼来，
　　　　花开引来蝴蝶舞，
　　　　有心引姐上歌台。

三　姐　（唱）
　　　　心想唱歌就唱歌，
　　　　心想撑船就下河，

Liu'er and Third Sister: Why, uncle, we haven't seen you for ages.

Old Fisherman: I've been out fishing for more than a month. As soon as I came ashore I heard you singing away, and that tells you must be somehow around.

Yaxiang: Third Sister, we're all waiting to match you in singing. Are you ready to be challenged?

Liu'er: Sister, I'll go home first.

Old Fisherman: Why don't you join the rest of us, Liu'er?

Liu'er: No, thanks. I'll fetch the firewood home first. Sister !

(*He draws Third Sister to one side.*)

(*wincing*) Shy away from touchy topics. Play safe. Venture not out of the comfort zone lest somebody might take offence.

Third Sister: There you go again. Always harping on your "playing safe" philosophy, brother. What do you mean by touchy topics, and whom could I offend?

(*Exit Liu'er.*)

Lanfen: Your brother is too good, you see.

All: Third Sister, come on and let us kick off our match.

Yamu (*heralding Third Sister*):

I'll take the lead.

Bees fly over the ridge for nectar;

Fish swarm into a rippling pool.

So let us applaud her premiere show.

Third Sister (*brimming with confidence*):

Sing to your heart's content,

Take to the river wherever you want to cast your net;

你拿竹篙我拿桨，

随你撑到哪条河。

亚　祥　（唱）

什么结子高又高？

什么结子半中腰？

什么结子成双对？

什么结子棒棒敲？

三　姐　（唱）

高粱结子高又高，

玉米结子半中腰，

豆角结子成双对，

收了芝麻棒棒敲。

众青年　（唱）

什么有嘴不讲话？

什么无嘴闹喳喳？

什么有脚不走路？

什么无脚走天涯？

兰　芬　（唱）

菩萨有嘴不讲话，

铜锣无嘴闹喳喳，

板凳有脚不走路，

……（一下答不上了。）

三　姐　（接唱）

大船无脚走天涯。

众欢笑。

Barge poles in your hands, net in mine,

I'll race you anywhere to the finish line.

Yaxiang (*trying one on her*)**:**

Take this riddle verse, to begin with.

What plant bears fruit at the top?

What does so in the middle?

What crop develops in pairs?

What sort of thing yields its seeds with a club?

Third Sister (*replying effortlessly*)**:**

Sorghum bears fruit at the top;

Maize is harvested in the middle;

And beans grow pods in pairs;

And sesame's seeds are gathered in by clubbing.

Young Men (*more riddle verses*)**:**

What has a mouth but speaks not?

What devoid of any mouth but speaks a lot?

What has feet but does not walk?

What without feet travels a lot?

Lanfen (*answering in her stead*)**:**

Bodhisattva has a mouth but speaks not;

Mouthless drums and gongs sound a lot;

Stools have feet but they don't walk;

(*She breaks off, at a loss.*)

Third Sister (*continuing*)**:**

A boat has none but travels far and wide.

(*They all laugh in glee.*)

众姑娘（唱）

　　　　什么结果抱娘颈？

　　　　什么结果一条心？

　　　　什么结果包梳子？

　　　　什么结果披鱼鳞？

三　姐（唱）

　　　　木瓜结果抱娘颈，

　　　　芭蕉结果一条心，

　　　　柚子结果包梳子，

　　　　菠萝结果披鱼鳞。

　　　（稍停，反问）

　　　　什么水面打筋斗？

　　　　什么水面起高楼？

　　　　什么水面撑雨伞？

　　　　什么水面共白头？

众青年（唱）

　　　　鸭子水面打筋斗，

　　　　大船水面起高楼，

　　　　荷叶水面撑雨伞，

　　　　鸳鸯水面共白头。

三　姐（唱）

　　　　什么大大四四方？

　　　　什么双双坐中堂？

　　　　什么样人常来往？

　　　　什么饱吞万担粮？

老渔翁（唱）

Girls (*continuing their word plays*):

> What plant has offspring clinging to its mother's neck?
>
> What plant comes to fruition clustered around one heart?
>
> What plant looks like a comb containing kernels inside?
>
> What plant bears fruit wrapped in scales?

Third Sister (*easily*):

> The papaya bears fruit clinging to its mother's neck;
>
> The banana bears fruit clustered around one heart;
>
> The pomelo bears fruit with combs as its separate parts;
>
> And the pineapple is wrapped in scales.
>
> (*After a pause, Third Sister teases them back with her share of riddle verses.*)
>
> What fowls spar upon the lake?
>
> What rises high on the river?
>
> What thereupon keeps out the sun?
>
> What water birds make a blessed pair?

Young men (*quick-witted*):

> Ducks spar upon the lake;
>
> Boats tower on the river;
>
> Lotus leaves blind the sun;
>
> Mandarin ducks make a model couple.

Third Sister (*more riddles*):

> What is roomy and square?
>
> What couple sits there?
>
> What kind of creatures trot to and fro?
>
> What devours whole tons of grain?

Old Fisherman (*singing*):

猪栏大大四四方，

兰芬、冬妹 （唱）

公猪母猪……

三　姐 （阻止兰、冬妹，另唱）

老爷奶奶坐中堂，

亚　祥 （唱）抢吃猪潲常来往，

三　姐 （唱）饱吞千家万担粮。

在盘歌时莫进财带着两名家丁，探头探脑地从众人后面过场。

老渔翁发现，他没有惊动众人，自己跟下去探视。

大家正唱得高兴，忽闻弓弦声，一只锦鸡落地，兰芬拾起。

众　人　锦鸡!

兰　芬　一定是小牛哥射的。

三　姐　你怎么知道?

兰　芬　听见弓声，锦鸡落地，除了小牛哥谁也不能。

亚　木　我们把它藏起来，让他找一找。

众　人　好。

三姐藏鸡。小牛身背弓箭上。

兰　芬　小牛哥，找什么?

小　牛　兰芬，你们看见一只锦鸡吗?

兰　芬　锦鸡?是有一只。

小　牛　是我射下来的。

三　姐　小牛，你射的锦鸡可有凭记?

小　牛　箭穿鸡颈正中。

三　姐　若不是呢?

The pigsty is roomy and square.

Lanfen and Dongmei (*singing*):

The hog and the sow...

Third Sister (*stopping them to sing herself*):

The landlord and his wife sit there.

Yaxiang: And devour whole tons of grain,

Third Sister: Robbed from countless homes!

(*Just then steward Mo and two servants sneak in. The old fisherman, without a word, retires.*)

(*Just then, the twang of a bow is heard and a pheasant falls to the ground. Lanfen picks it up.*)

All: A pheasant!

Lanfen: Must be brother Xiaoniu's game!

Third Sister: How do you know?

Lanfen: The bow twanged and the pheasant fell. No one is a better marksman than him.

Yamu: Let's play hide-and-seek game with him.

All: All right.

(*Third Sister hides the pheasant. Enter Xiaoniu with bow and arrows.*)

Lanfen: What are you looking for, Xiaoniu?

Xiaoniu: Have you seen a pheasant, Lanfen?

Lanfen: What if I did?

Xiaoniu: It's one I shot down.

Third Sister: What proof have you, Xiaoniu, that you shot it?

Xiaoniu: As a rule, the arrow goes through the middle of its neck.

Third Sister: If not?

小　牛　那就不是我射的。

兰　芬　拿来大家看。

三　姐　（拿出锦鸡）不前不后，正中当中。

亚　木　小牛哥真是神箭手。

　　　　　众欢笑，三姐把鸡递还小牛。

小　牛　这只锦鸡就送给二哥吧。

兰　芬　（憨直地）小牛哥，你总是送给二哥，为什么不送给三姐？

春　姐　蠢妹子，他嘴上说给二哥，心里是给三姐！

兰　芬　三姐，真的吗？

　　　　　众哄笑，小牛不好意思跑下，韦老奶挑茶上。

韦老奶　喝茶啰！（唱）

　　　　　挑来一担神仙露，

　　　　　老人喝了寿命长，

　　　　　后生喝了配织女，

　　　　　姑娘喝了配牛郎。

　　　　　众笑，小牛手拿一块写有"莫"字的木牌上。

小　牛　你们看这是什么？

兰　芬　莫海仁的"莫"字，圩场上、地头上到处插着这种牌子，哪个不
　　　　认得。

　　　　　老渔翁暗上。

Xiaoniu: Then it's not mine.

Lanfen: Bring it out and let's have a check.

Third Sister (*producing the pheasant*): Nice shot indeed. Exactly through the middle.

Yamu: Hurrah! Brother Xiaoniu is certainly a crack shot.

(*They all congratulate Xiaoniu as Third Sister returns the bird to him.*)

Xiaoniu: I'd like to gift it to brother Liu'er.

Lanfen (*innocently*): Xiaoniu, why do you always give presents to Liu'er? Why not to Third Sister?

Chunjie: A dense girl! Everybody can tell what a good pretender Xiaoniu is except you.

Lanfen: Is that true, Third Sister?

(*They all laugh as Xiaoniu hurries off in embarrassment. Enter Grandma Wei with a kettle of tea.*)

Grandma Wei: Come and have a cup of tea, all of you. (*lovingly*)

Here's a kettle of magic nectar here,

Which works wonder to give long life to the old;

Young men who drink it marry the lasses they dream of,

Girls, the lads they love tender and true.

(*They all laugh. Enter Xiaoniu holding a wooden placard with a character "Mo" on it.*)

Xiaoniu (*espying an irregularity*): Look at this!

Lanfen: That's a notice placard reading "Mo" for Lord Mo Hairen. There are a plenty planted all over the market-places and the fields. Who doesn't know it?

(*The old fisherman comes on imperceptibly.*)

小　牛	怎么插到我们茶山来了呢？
韦老奶	莫非他又要霸占茶山？
老渔翁	对，莫海仁要霸占这座山！
三　姐	老公公，你怎么晓得？
老渔翁	方才莫海仁在山脚下，朝着山上指手画脚，对莫进财讲了几句，骑马就走。
三　姐	他讲什么？

老渔翁 （念）

　　莫家在此，

　　安葬祖坟，

　　从今天起，

　　封山禁林。

小　牛　莫海仁这个狗贼子……

三　姐 （唱）

　　众人天，众人地，

　　众人河川众人山，

　　众人茶林众人管，

　　与他莫家不相干。

韦老奶 （唱）

　　开天辟地到如今，

　　未曾见过禁山林，

小　牛 （唱）

　　谁人敢把茶山禁，

　　一箭要他命归阴！

中年人　莫家财多势大，和官府常来常往，你怎能斗得过他？

Xiaoniu: Why are there so many notices stuck up in the tea plantations?

Grandma Wei: Does that mean he plots to take the plantations too?

Old Fisherman: Yes! Mo Hairen sets his eyes on our livelihood.

Third Sister: How do you know, uncle?

Old Fisherman: Just now Lord Mo came to the foot of the hill. He talked to his steward before riding off.

Third Sister: What did he say?

Old Fisherman (*imitating Lord Mo's morose and avaricious tone*):

Be it known:

Upon this very hill the Mo's ancestral graves lie;

From today onwards the hill is out of bounds;

And no more wood cutting is allowed!

Xiaoniu: That rascal Mo Hairen!

Third Sister (*protesting*):

Earth belongs to us all, a piece of common sense.

So is the heaven, everybody's source of livelihood.

Indiscriminately rivers and mountains sustain humanity.

Tea plantations are wrought with each laboring hand,

Beyond the pale and reach of the local tyrant.

Grandma Wei (*firmly*):

Since the creation of earth and heaven,

Who ever heard of a mountain put out of bounds?

Xiaoniu (*ranting*):

Let any man claim this hill to be his property——

My arrow thinks otherwise!

A Middle-aged Man (*submissively*): This hereditary overlord called Mo has

三　姐（唱）

　　　　一根木柴难起火，

　　　　柴多火苗高过天，

　　　　只要穷人同心意，

　　　　不怕莫家霸茶山。

　　　　众合唱后两句。

　　　　莫进财与二家丁复上。

莫进财　你们讲什么？（念）

　　　　此乃龙山宝林，

　　　　老爷要葬祖坟，

　　　　你等弄刀动斧，

　　　　神龙必定受惊，

　　　　伤龙龙口喷火，

　　　　全村灾难来临，

　　　　老爷今日有命，

　　　　严禁采茶伐林。

三　姐　哼！（唱）

　　　　西山原是荒山岭，

　　　　不见茶树不见林，

　　　　问你莫家那时节，

power and influence. Even the magistrate defers to him one way or another. This is the principal fact of our existence here. We'd better try our best not to be implicated in any trouble or incur his displeasure.

Third Sister (*iconoclastically*):

One fagot does not make a bonfire;

When everybody adds some fuel, the flames will rise.

United, we stand to prevail for sure,

And thwart any scheme of the Mo family to steal our crop.

(*All join in singing the last two lines.*)

(*Re-enter the steward with two servants.*)

Steward: What the hell you're arguing here? (*sensing a certain tension in the air*)

At the behest of my master, I am here to announce,

Lord Mo alone is entitled to the ownership of this hill,

Since, you must all note, this is a dragon hill;

Where the Mos have interred ancestors;

Any human activity like chopping and hacking wood,

Is prone to disturb the spirit of the sacred dragon;

Which will spurt fire if disturbed;

To the extent calamity will overtake the whole village.

So our master has decided to ban;

Various human actions including wood cutting and tea picking.

Third Sister: Bah! (*indignantly*)

This western hill used to be no-man's land,

Bare of any vegetation, shrub or plant of real worth.

Nowadays you claim this clot to be your ancestral burial ground.

不葬祖坟为何情？

西山如今会生财，

全因穷人把茶栽，

一片茶叶一滴汗，

莫家强抢该不该？

众　人（唱）

不该，不该，大不该，

莫家强抢大不该！

莫进财　众位父老兄弟，莫老爷为了全村人的吉祥平安，特地请来风水
先生，他们讲，西山原是生龙口……

小　牛　呸！（唱）

若然这是生龙口，

我们早有绫罗穿；

撕下莫家鬼脸壳，

封山原是为霸山。

莫进财　穷有穷命，富有富命，老爷要葬祖坟，这乃天注定，怎么说是
霸山？

三　姐（唱）

不是命，不是天，

莫家有把铁算盘，

莫家算盘一声响，

（把）穷人关进鬼门关！

莫进财　刘三姐你吃了豹子胆，竟敢骂起莫老爷来了。

三　姐（唱）

Why did you not inter your deceased there by then?

Today the western hill has become a treasure trove,

Thanks to our constant toiling it into thriving tea plantations.

Mark every piece of tea leave is soaked with a drop of our sweat;

Such incongruous demand is anti-climax to say the least.

All (*protesting*):

They are not justified at all to take away our livelihood!

The Mo family has no right to denude us of this hill!

Steward (*putting on airs*): Good folk, to ensure the communal stability, my lord makes a point to consult geomancers, who say that the western hill is the dragon's mouth that everybody should never tread upon.

Xiaoniu: Rot! (*rebuking him*)

If this village were a dragon's mouth,

We'd have been wearing silk since long ago;

Off with Mo's devilish mask.

You seal it simply to rob us of it.

Steward (*impudently*): There is no arguing fate. If my lord decides this hill is his ancestral graveyard, I construe it to be heaven's decree. How can you characterize it robbery?

Third Sister (*straight to the point*):

Avoid the maudlin.

We are not born impoverished,

Neither fate ordains us such a litany of woes,

When all our grievances issue from a shrew abacus.

Steward: Reckless and churlish! Third Sister, you dare curse our master?

Third Sister (*chortling*):

上山有棍打得蛇，

下水有网捉得鳖，

有理敢把皇帝骂，

管你老爷不老爷！

众　人（唱）

有理敢把皇帝骂，

管你老爷不老爷！

莫进财　好啊！刘三姐，你几次唆使土民与莫老爷作对，你等着看吧！

（狼狈地边说边欲下，绊在一块大石头上，几乎跌倒。）

众人大笑。

莫进财　你们这些穷骨头，莫高兴得这样早，这山早晚是莫老爷的。

三　姐　莫进财，你说这山是莫老爷的，你为什么不帮他搬回家去？

小　牛（举起大石头）还有这块大石头！给你！

莫进财惊慌失措。

兰　芬　哎哎！还有这块破木牌。（顺手向莫进财掷去。）

莫进财　刘三姐，你小心点，你小心点！（下。）

三　姐　兄妹们，我们还是采茶砍柴去！

——幕落

We handle snakes on the hill with a stick,

Cast a net to catch turtles in the river;

Being in the right we dare curse the emperor,

Let alone an overlord like yours!

All (*chortling*):

Being in the right we dare curse the emperor,

Let alone an overlord like yours!

Steward (*suddenly becoming very nasty*): You have got your facts wrong, Third Sister! This isn't the first time you've caused disturbance. Just you wait!

(*Retiring in chagrin as he talks, he trips over a rock. The villagers are convulsed in laughter.*)

Steward (*menacingly*): Don't laugh too soon, you rag-tags! This hill is the property of my lord very soon.

Third Sister: That being the case, why don't you shoulder it to and fro?

Xiaoniu (*picking up a big stone*): Here's a rock for you too. There!

(*The Steward finds himself in sore straits.*)

Lanfen: Yes, and take this broken placard of yours. (*She throws it at the Steward. All the young people laugh heartily.*)

Steward (*humiliated*): Enough is enough! Third Sister! You have got to find out what is what before you start stirring up all this trouble. I will report on you.(*Exit.*)

Third Sister: Sheer act of bravado. Let's go on cutting firewood and picking tea, brothers and sisters.

(*Curtain.*)

第三场　定计

时　　紧接上场。

地　　莫海仁家二堂，雕梁画栋，帷幕低垂。

　　　　四个丫鬟随莫海仁上，内有一丫鬟手捧金丝鸟笼，内中装的是
　　　　莫海仁爱如珍宝的鹩哥。

莫海仁　（念）

　　　　良田万顷我嫌少，

　　　　老婆九个不嫌多。

　　　　我，莫海仁，可恨那些穷骨头叫我"谋害人"。哼！只要年年粮
　　　　谷满仓，岁岁黄金万两，管他海仁还是害人。（笑。坐，逗弄笼
　　　　中鹩哥，教他学话）黄金……万两……妻妾……满堂。

　　　　鹩哥学得极像，莫海仁大笑。

莫进财　（上）见过老爷

莫海仁　进财回来了，封山禁林之事可曾办好？

莫进财　老爷呀！（唱）

　　　　奉了老爷命，

　　　　前去禁山林，

　　　　山上众穷鬼，

ACT THREE
An Evil Plan Is Hatched

Time: Shortly after the last scene.

Venue: The inner quarters of Lord Mo Hairen's mansion, with carved beams, painted pillars and long curtains.

(*Enter four maids in attendance on Mo Hairen. One carries a gilded cage with his pet parrot in it.*)

Lord Mo (*rather pleased with himself*):

A proprietor of extensive estate, a citizen of solid wealth,

And a husband of nine wives.

I am Mo Hairen. Those poor bastards call me Mo the Murderer. Confound them! But so long as my barns bulge with rice and I roll in gold and silver coins each year, I don't care they call me a benefactor or murderer.

(*He sits down tittering and plays with the parrot in the cage, teaching it to talk.*)

"Mountains of gold, women in plenty..."

(*He sniggers watching the parrot mimics him slavishly.*)

(*Enter the steward.*)

Steward (*bowing*): Sir!

Lord Mo (*curtly*): So you're back. What is it that vexes you so much?

Steward: Ah, sir! (*whining*)

I did proclaim your express injunction as ordered, sir;

But the wretched riffraff keeps on cutting wood and picking tea there;

They have dismantled our notice placards,

砍柴采茶闹纷纷，

禁牌被拔掉，

开口还骂人，

他说老爷你……

莫海仁　怎么样？

莫进财　（唱）封山原为霸山林。

莫海仁　什么人如此大胆？

莫进财　（唱）

为首就是刘三姐。

莫海仁　又是那刘三姐！

莫进财　她唆使刁民，不许，（唱）

不许莫家霸山林。

莫海仁　这个黄毛丫头，三番五次与我作对，我恨不得将她……

莫进财　将刘三姐一刀……

莫海仁　不可……想那刘三姐深得人心，远近闻名，若是将她杀死，那
些穷鬼岂肯罢休？

莫进财　赶她出境！

莫海仁　岂不太便宜了这个丫头。

莫进财　杀既不能，赶又不好，难道就这样罢了不成！

莫海仁眼望笼中鹩哥，沉思不语。

莫进财　老爷，刘三姐不除，终是心腹大患。

And started reviling us and accusing you, sir.

Lord Mo: Of what?

Steward (*singing*):

　　Of putting the hill out of bounds!

Lord Mo: Who was so insolent?

Steward (*viciously*):

　　Initial checkup reveals the ring-leader is Third Sister;

　　As she is the most contentious and vocal in the brawl.

Lord Mo: The brat again!

Steward (*viciously*):

　　She is so inflammatory that she fouls things up, as usual.

　　I mean, our plan to take the tea plantations aborted.

Lord Mo (*grinding his teeth*): The little bitch has crossed my path time and again. Damned if I don't...

Steward: Kill her!

Lord Mo (*craftily*): No. She is too popular. We must handle with care. If I kill her, those beggars won't take it lying down.

Steward: Banish her out of this district then.

Lord Mo: That would be too lenient for her extravagant affront.

Steward (*baffled*): If we can't kill her, drive her out, are we going to let her get away with this?

　　(*Mo Hairen is deeply lost in thoughts while gazing at the parrot in the cage.*)

Steward: If she stays on, sir, she'll be a thorn in our flesh.

鹩哥叫。

莫海仁　（阴笑几声）进财，你看。（念）鸟儿进了金丝笼，谅她有翅膀难
　　　　飞腾。

莫进财　（会意地）笼——中——鸟。

莫海仁　自古道，"射人先射马，擒贼先擒王"，这样既可封住她的嘴，又
　　　　可离间她和众刁民。快去把王媒婆请来。

莫进财　老爷远见，老爷高才！（下。）

　　　　——幕落

(*The parrot squawks.*)

Lord Mo (*with a chuckle of delight*): Look, steward!

Put a bird in a gilded cage,

And even with wings she can't fly!

Steward (*taking the hint*): A... caged...bird.

Lord Mo (*craftily*): There is an old saying, "Aim at the rider's horse. The king of brigands first to justice bring." This is the way to neutralize her influence and cut her off from the rest of the mob. Send the matchmaker Mmes. Wang here at once!

Steward (*smiling obsequiously*): What stratagem you have up in your sleeves, sir!

(*Exit.*)

(*Curtain.*)

第四场　拒婚

中幕前，上场的次日，王媒婆捧着莫家聘礼上。

媒　婆（唱）
　　三寸舌头一嘴油，
　　男婚女嫁把我求。
　　哄得狐狸团团转，
　　哄得孔雀配斑鸠。

　　我，王媒婆，一不耕田，二不种地，专靠做媒为生，昨日奉了莫老爷之命，要我到刘三姐家去说媒。（唱）

　　刘家丫头谁不晓，
　　人又刁蛮嘴又嚣。
　　不是路边闲花草，
　　她是高山红辣椒。（想）
　　嘿！我王媒婆也不是好惹的咧！一来看在银子分上，而来凭着老娘这张利嘴，也要去试她一试。（唱）

　　白银子来黑眼睛，
　　只认银子不认人，
　　只要银子拿到手，
　　哪管天理与良心。

ACT FOUR
Matchmaker on Her Fool's Errand

Time: The next day.

Venue: In front of the inner curtain.

(Enter the matchmaker Mmes. Wang, bringing along Lord Mo's gifts.)

Matchmaker (*with unconscious complacency*):

A matchmaker, I have glib lip,

My craft becomes my purse with recommen-dations more artistic than honest,

I can trick a fox into dancing,

Or a peacock into mating with a turtle-dove.

Call me Wang. Matchmaking is my trade. Yesterday Lord Mo sent me to his mansion. He made me to call on Third Sister with an offer of marriage. (*musing*)

Here is the village beauty and more, special to tout,

Sharp of wit, quick of tongue, she's got all sorts of fetching ways;

Neither a roadside flower nor common clay,

Such pleasantries blossom forth in a rural setting rarely.

Hmm, I am an old hand. I'll use my ready tongue to have a try, if only for the sake of such an unromantic but rich character like Lord Mo. (*rakishly*)

My eyes are black; silver is white.

Money is the only care that I care.

Just let my hands be laid on silver,

And away with good sense and human feeling!

媒婆下。

——中幕启

时　　　接过场

景　　　刘二家门口，两株木瓜树，一架瓜棚，一排竹篱。

　　　　三姐正在绣着箭袋，边绣边唱。

三　姐　（唱）

绣只蝴蝶采鲜花，

绣个葫芦配金瓜，

绣条蛟龙腾云起，

绣个箭袋送给他。（韦老奶与兰芬上，三姐并未发现，仍唱）

金丝绣袋送给哥，

装满利箭挂身旁，

望哥箭箭不空放，

韦老奶　（唱）

射尽世间虎与狼。

兰　芬　（拿过箭袋，故作不知地）哟！原来是个箭袋呀！

韦老奶　小心！莫弄脏了，这是三姐送人用的。

兰　芬　三姐你送哪个，送哪个？

三　姐　哪里，外婆讲笑。

韦老奶　什么？外婆讲笑？！

兰　芬　绣得真好呀！三姐，你教我绣。

韦老奶　你绣箭袋，送给哪一个？

(*Exit.*)

(*The inner curtain rises.*)

Time: Immediately after.

Venue: The yard in front of Liu'er's house with two papaya trees, a melon trellis and a bamboo fence.

(*Third Sister is humming a tune while embroidering a quiver.*)

Third Sister (*humming a tune*):

This quiver sewn with golden threads is my special gift for him.

With which my love sets out on a hunting out;

(*Enter Grandma Wei and Lanfen. Third Sister does not see them and sings on.*)

May he never miss his prey,

May he slay all the wolves and tigers in the world!

Grandma Wei (*suggestively*):

Yes. All the wolves and tigers in the world!

Lanfen (*snatching the quiver and pretending not to know for whom it is intended*): Ah, it's a quiver!

Grandma Wei: Be careful! Don't soil it. Third Sister is making a present for someone.

Lanfen: Who's this for, Third Sister?

Third Sister (*crimsoning*): No one. Granny was teasing.

Grandma Wei: What? Teasing, was I?

Lanfen: Beautiful handiwork, isn't it? You must teach me to embroider too, Third Sister.

Grandma Wei (*jestingly*): Who is the lucky boy to get your quiver when you

兰　芬　奶奶，看你就喜欢笑人，我……我……我哪个也不送，一生一世
　　　　就跟着三姐。（唱）
　　　　姐是明月妹是星，
　　　　有星无月天不明，
　　　　妹愿跟姐永做伴，
　　　　如同星星伴月行。
　　　　老渔翁、小牛先后上。

韦老奶　（笑唱）
　　　　棒槌吹火不通气，
　　　　姐妹怎比月和星？
　　　　三姐同你永作伴，
　　　　莫非小牛打单身？
　　　　小牛听韦老奶唱后害羞欲走，被老渔翁拦住。

老渔翁　（唱）
　　　　山中只有藤缠树，
　　　　世上哪有树缠藤；
　　　　青藤若是不缠树，
　　　　枉过一春又一春。

兰　芬　三姐，为什么只有藤缠树，没有树缠藤呢？

老渔翁　兰芬，你还不去捡猪菜？

兰　芬　（会意）呵，老公公，你也该打鱼去了。

embroider one?

Lanfen (*blushing scarlet*): What a tease you are, granny. I... I... I won't give it to

anyone. I'll keep the company of Third Sister all my life. (*resolving*)

Third Sister is the moon, I but one of the stars;

The moon always bulks large in the sky.

I mean to be her life long female confidante;

Like a myriad of stars attending the major light.

(*Enter the old fisherman with a basket and net on his back.*)

Grandma Wei (*breaking a jest with Lanfen*):

You are blowing at the fire through a rolling pin!

Xiaoniu is all her heart has room for.

Don't you butt in between them;

That is not Third Sister's idea at all.

(*Xiaoniu enters in time to hear Grandma Wei's song. He turns to go, but is*

stopped by the old fisherman.)

Old Fisherman (*sublimely*):

Banyan trees must be entwined,

Vines must cling to banyan trees;

No earthly couples remain more loyal,

For the spring is meant for such a nice end.

Lanfen (*all innocence*): Third Sister, why must vines cling to banyan trees, and

not the other way round?

Old Fisherman: Lanfen, aren't you going to get vegetables for the pigs in the

pen?

Lanfen (*taking the hint*): Oh, yes, I must get going. Aren't you hitting to the

river fishing, grandpa?

老渔翁　啊！打鱼去！

兰　芬　小牛哥，这是三姐送给你的箭袋。

　　　　　兰芬与韦老奶下。

老渔翁　小牛，下水容易，上水难啰。老汉打鱼去啦！哈哈……（下。）

小　牛　（唱）

　　　　　新买水缸栽莲藕，

　　　　　莲藕开花朵朵鲜；

　　　　　金丝蚂蚁缸边转，

　　　　　隔水难得近花前。

三　姐　（唱）

　　　　　对河只有鹭鸶鸟，

　　　　　眼睛明亮翅膀尖；

　　　　　有心飞过连天水，

　　　　　莫怕山高水连天。

小牛、三姐　（唱）

　　　　　连就连。

　　　　　我俩结交订百年；

　　　　　哪个九十七岁死，

　　　　　奈何桥上等三年。

　　　　　三姐给小牛挂箭袋，小牛把手镯送给三姐。兰芬与数男女青年
　　　　　暗上。

小牛、三姐　（唱）

　　　　　风吹云动天不动，

　　　　　水推船移天不移；

　　　　　刀切莲藕丝不断，

Old Fisherman: Why, yes, I must be off.

Lanfen: Brother Xiaoniu, have a look at the quiver Third Sister has made you.

> (*Lanfen and Grandma Wei leave.*)

Old Fisherman: It's easier to sail downstream than upstream, Xiaoniu, I'm off now to fish. Hoho! (*Exit.*)

Xiaoniu (*with a meaningful look at her*):

> I bought a new water tank in which to plant some lotus roots,
>
> And watch them sprout into a parade of ruddy petals;
>
> Luring a pack of golden ants to trot around the rim,
>
> But water keeps them from the flowers.

Third Sister (*tenderly*):

> Across the river tiptoes a cormorant,
>
> Bright of eyes, sharp of wings,
>
> Eager to fly over the river.
>
> That eagerness will overcome all the barriers.

Xiaoniu and Third Sister (*with a rapt expression on both faces*):

> Hand in hand, heart to heart.
>
> We are a happy couple so long as we live.
>
> Storms cannot quench our passion;
>
> Rivers cannot wash our love away.
>
> (*Third Sister fastens the quiver on Xiaoniu, who gives her a bracelet. Lanfen and some other young people tiptoe in.*)

Xiaoniu and Third Sister (*affectionately*):

> The wind scatters the clouds but not the sky,
>
> The river moves the boat but not the shore;
>
> Filaments still link the lotus root cut off,

斧砍江水水不离。

众重唱，小牛含羞下。刘二担水上，众下，三姐拿锄头欲下地干活。

刘　二　又是什么刀切、斧砍的。

三　姐　二哥。（亮亮手镯。）

刘　二　（未发现）三妹，你们又唱些什么？前天在茶山上，莫管家的话你没有忘记吧？

三　姐　没有忘呵，他说要我小心点。

刘　二　没忘记就好，我下地干活去了。（从三姐手中夺过锄头。）

三　姐　二哥。（拿草帽挂在刘二身上。）

刘　二　你在家好好纺纱，不要出去砍柴了。（下。）

三　姐　二哥，你要早去早回呵。（纺棉纱。）

媒婆手拿聘礼上。

媒　婆　哟！三女儿呀，三女儿！你真是聪明能干呵！

三　姐　（唱）

亲手种棉亲手纺，

自己织布自己穿，

三姐不爱人夸奖，

花言巧语莫来谈。

媒　婆　不是妈妈夸奖，像你这样才貌双全，将来定享大福。

Chop a stream, it keeps flowing.

(*The young people join in. Xiaoniu goes out. Enter Liu'er carrying water. The young people leave. Third Sister picks up a hoe to go to the fields.*)

Liu'er: What is all this about ominous words like swords and axe in your songs?

Third Sister: Does that irk you again? Brother! (*She points to her bracelet but he does not see it.*)

Liu'er (*apprehensively*): Yes. It does. What Lord Mo's steward intimated the other day in the tea plantations is no empty words, I assure you.

Third Sister: So what? He has blackmailed me. They will move further against me.

Liu'er: We have had one patch of bad luck after another. Keep this fact in perspective. Well, I have still got farm work in the fields. (*He takes the hoe from her.*)

Third Sister: Brother! (*She hands him his straw hat.*)

Liu'er: You'd better stay at home spinning. Forget about firewood today. (*Exit.*)

Third Sister: All right, take care, brother.

(*Third Sister starts spinning. The matchmaker enters with the gifts.*)

Matchmaker (*smiling her most winning smile*): Ah, my dear, what a clever, capable girl you are!

Third Sister (*proclaiming*):

With my own hands I plant and spin the yarns;

With my own hands I weave the clothes I wear.

Third Sister dislikes snobbery intensely;

Save your honeyed tongue for elsewhere, not lavishing it on me.

Matchmaker: Aunty isn't flattering you. With your beauty and homemaking

三　姐　（唱）

天大福气不稀罕，

三姐偏偏爱种田，

从小生来有双手，

哪愁吃来哪愁穿。

媒　婆　三女儿，你哥哥呢?

三　姐　我哥哥哪有你清闲，他下地干活去了。

媒　婆　三女儿，我是来向你兄妹两个道喜的呀!

三　姐　王妈妈，什么喜呀!

媒　婆　三女儿，看你聪明一世，懵懂一时哟！你唱得一口好歌，又长得如花似朵，东西南北，远远近近，谁个不知，哪个不晓。（观看三姐神色，不敢直言）三女儿，你的时运来了，本村莫……莫……莫老爷。

三　姐　莫老爷有良田万顷。

媒　婆　是呀，是呀!

三　姐　莫老爷有家财万贯。

媒　婆　对啰，对啰!

三　姐　莫老爷家吃的是山珍海味。

媒　婆　是呀！是呀!

三　姐　莫老爷家穿的是绫罗绸缎。

skills, great things are in store ahead!

Third Sister (*unwaveringly*):

> Good fortune and windfall wealth prove no lure to me;
>
> I take pride in providing for myself working the fields;
>
> I was born with a pair of hands that work, and a brain that thinks;
>
> The last thing I wish is to be somebody's dependent.

Matchmaker: Where is your brother, my dear?

Third Sister (*coldly*): He has this family of us to provide for—— he's working in the fields.

Matchmaker: I've come to congratulate you both, dear.

Third Sister: Why should you congratulate us, Mmes. Wang?

Matchmaker (*smugly*): Dear, clever as you are, how can you be so dummy? You're the district songbird and the village beauty. You evolve such a fame across the country. (*Receiving no encouragement, she dares not speak outright.*) You're in luck, dearest! Mr. Mo... Lord Mo as you know...

Third Sister (*pretending to be at sea*): You mean the largest proprietor in the neighborhood.

Matchmaker: That's right, that's right!

Third Sister (*sarcastically*): Legend also say he is the most distinguished man of wealth and position.

Matchmaker: Just so, just so!

Third Sister (*continuing her horseplay*): His family live such high lifestyles that is truly the envy of us all.

Matchmaker: That's right, that's right!

Third Sister (*suggestively*): They all dress in brocade and silk, scrubbed to their very best every day.

媒　婆　对啰，对啰！（唱）

　　　　家财万贯且不讲，

三　姐　（唱）

　　　　奶奶太太有九房，

媒　婆　（唱）

　　　　大小九个不生养。

三　姐　（唱）

　　　　但愿人间绝虎狼。

媒　婆　（唱）

　　　　进财找我好几趟，

三　姐　（唱）

　　　　你想说媒我相帮。

媒　婆　三女儿呀，三女儿，你真乖呵！

三　姐　不知莫老爷又想找哪一个！

媒　婆　这个……（唱）

　　　　一要人品最风流，

三　姐　（接唱）二要能说又会讲。

媒　婆　（唱）三要远近都闻名，

三　姐　（唱）四要才貌都相当。

媒　婆　远在天边，近在……

三　姐　近在眼前！（指媒婆，唱）

　　　　看你人品最风流，

Matchmaker: Just so, just so. (*cringing*)

> My most respected client also is known to have raked in the largest volumes of gold and silver far and near.

Third Sister (*satirically*):

> On top of that, an owner of a bevy of nine wives and concubines too!

Matchmaker (*concernedly*):

> Pity is that all his nine wives have sired no descendants to inherit his property.

Third Sister (*scornfully*):

> May all tigers and wolves perish from the earth!

Matchmaker (*in all earnestness*):

> His steward has visited me several times lately.

Third Sister (*mockingly*):

> If you want me to make a match, I'll help you.

Matchmaker (*carried away by her eloquence*): My dear, dear girl, how intelligent you are!

Third Sister: With whom is Lord Mo besotted this time?

Matchmaker: Well. (*She sings.*)

> First she must have charm.

Third Sister (*singing*): Second, a ready tongue.

Matchmaker (*singing*): Third, a name known far and near.

Third Sister (*singing*): Fourth, talent and beauty to match.

Matchmaker (*with a smirk*): You could say she is as far as the distant horizon, or as near as...

Third Sister (*coming to the climax of her jibe*): Talk of the devils (*Pointing to the matchmaker, she sings.*)

扭扭捏捏到处游；

看你能说又会讲，

好比癫狗吠日头；

看你名声传得远，

臭名鼎鼎盖九州；

看你才貌两相当，

黄牙白眼一嘴油。

你同老爷两相配，

好比山猪配花猴。

烧香谢天又谢地，

送你鬼婆出门楼。

媒　婆　呸！刘三姐，你可不要狗咬吕洞宾，不知好人心哪！

刘二扛着锄头上。小牛和几个男女青年陆续上。

三　姐　（唱）

好篮从来不装灰，

好人从来不做媒，

今天碰着刘三姐，

红薯落灶你该煨。

刘　二　三妹，什么事？

媒　婆　刘二，莫老爷看上了你家三姐，老娘好心好意前来说媒……

三　姐　（念）

给你大路九十九，

You surely charm everybody,

With the readiest tongue ever known,

Becoming modesty is the least of your virtues.

But your fame travels far and wide,

A legend throughout the country.

Your talent and beauty prove so irresistible,

That Lord Mo even condescends to propose your hand.

My sixth sense tells me you two make an ideal pair,

We shall burn incense to thank heaven and earth,

For a superb union of beauty and wealth.

Matchmaker: Holy heaven! Third Sister! I am not a good woman to get on the wrong side of. Think you are somebody? To have hoaxed me in public?

(*Enter Liu'er with his hoe, followed by Xiaoniu and several other young people.*)

Third Sister (*at a total impasse*):

A good basket will not carry rubbish,

Neither will a good woman be a Matchmaker with shady reputation.

Today, up against our tough sister,

You're grilled like a wretched potato.

Liu'er: What's the matter, sister?

Matchmaker: Liu'er, Lord Mo has taken a fancy to your sister. He bothers himself to ask me to call on you...

Third Sister (*eager to rid her of the matter*):

You have ninety-nine roads before you,

　　　　　叫声媒婆你快走。

媒　婆　（念）

　　　　　老爷等你开金口，

　　　　　婚事不成我不走。

三　姐　（念）

　　　　　山中狼虎我见过，

　　　　　难道还怕一条狗！

刘　二　（拿过聘礼给媒婆）王妈妈，自古道，竹门对竹门，木门对木门，
　　　　　这门亲事我不敢高攀。

青年群众　快走！

小　牛　（唱）

　　　　　老刁骡，

　　　　　背起东西往回驮，

　　　　　我赶刁骡赶得怪，

　　　　　不打屁股专打脚。

　　　　　众笑。

媒　婆　好。你兄妹不知好歹……你等着……你……

　　　　　莫进财上，踩着媒婆的脚。

媒　婆　哎哟，哪个砍头鬼！（抬头一看是莫进财，忙转笑脸。）

　　　　　莫进财回头请莫海仁及家丁上。

Make the smart choice and get out quickly!

Matchmaker (*boldfaced*):

Lord Mo is kind to offer to marry you;

I shall not leave until the match is made.

Third Sister (*making a wry face*):

Wolves and tigers are a common sight in the wild,

You are about as welcome as a skewer through the eye!

Liu'er (*evasively, returning the gifts to the matchmaker*): Mmes. Wang, I am afraid this is a mismatched offer as we are so much inferior in social status. So runs an old proverb: A bamboo door matches a bamboo door. And a wooden gate suits a wooden gate. Simple as that. What have we done to deserve such an honor?

Young men: Be off now, double quick!

Xiaoniu (*heaving a sigh of relief, gloatingly*):

Stubborn old mule,

Trot away with your burden on your back.

I have my way spurring wicked beasts——

Not whipping their rump but their legs!

(*There is an uproar.*)

Matchmaker (*thoroughly browbeaten, yet firing a parting shot*): Very well. what's good for you...You must learn the ways of the world the hard way. Just wait... Just wait.

(*Enter the steward who steps on the matchmaker's foot.*)

Matchmaker: Ouch! What filthy imbecile... (*Looking up to see the steward, she puts on a smiling face.*)

(*The steward turns to greet Lord Mo Hairen, entering with his servants.*)

莫进财　　刘二，莫老爷亲自看你兄妹来了。

媒　婆　　刘三姐，莫老爷亲自来了，你有什么话，就同老爷讲吧！

刘　二　　莫老爷来了，你看这里也没个坐处。

莫海仁　　（伪善地）刘二，你的病好了没有？莫某事务繁忙，过去照顾不
　　　　　　到，今后嘛……

莫进财　　今后你们要是靠上莫家这棵大树，那就风吹不怕，雨打不惊了。

三　姐　　（唱）

　　　　　　别处财主要我死，

　　　　　　这里财主要我活；

　　　　　　往日只见锅煮饭，

　　　　　　今天看见饭煮锅。

　　　　　　群众哄笑。

刘　二　　老爷请莫见怪，我三妹性情执拗，不敢……

莫海仁　　不！你三妹聪明过人，若能陪伴老爷，那我就称心如意了。

刘　二　　我们家贫命苦，实在不敢高攀！

莫进财　　刘二，你不要不识抬举，你莫忘记了你种的是莫老爷的田，吃
　　　　　　的是莫老爷的饭！若还惹恼了莫老爷，收回你的田地……

三　姐　　（唱）

　　　　　　他要收田由他收，

　　　　　　三姐饿死不低头，

Steward: Liu'er, Lord Mo has come in person to see you and your sister.

Matchmaker: Third Sister, my master has paid a visit to you in person. Tell him how much you are pleased with the offer.

Liu'er: Mr. Mo! I'm sorry we haven't even a chair in the house.

Lord Mo (*hypocritically*): Never mind. What has ailed you, Liu'er? I have been so busy of late. In future, though...

Steward (*echoing his master's feigned solicitude*): In future, you will be brought into his patronage and you will be free from any want of woes.

Third Sister (*with a sardonic smile*):

> The wicked and the rich elsewhere have pestered me to death,
>
> But here they want me to thrive;
>
> Normally stoves are used to cook rice,
>
> Today it seems the rice is cooking the stove instead!

(*Another uproar is rising from the young people.*)

Liu'er: Please don't bother her, sir. My sister gets too easily in bad mood...

Lord Mo: Well, well! Proper manners the lass's got, hasn't she? Your sister is smart though. I shall be very happy if she will take my hand and be my woman.

Liu'er (*conciliatorily*): We are overwhelmed, but I wonder if this is utterly beneath you. We really cannot aspire to such distinction.

Steward (*imperiously*): Take this offer graciously, Liu'er. Mark you are one of his tenants. If you cross his path, I am afraid he'll recoup the land you have rented...

Third Sister (*disdainfully but distinctly*):

> Let him evict us the way he does,
>
> I'd sooner starve to death than toady to him;

多少人家无田地，

砍柴一样度春秋。

莫进财　打开天窗说亮话，刘二，你到底答应不答应？

刘　二　还是请老爷另选高门吧！

莫海仁　你既不应承，这也没什么，进财……

莫进财　（拿出算盘算账）刘二，你去年治病借的银子，利加利，利滚利，本利共欠一十五两二钱七。

莫海仁　马上还清！

莫进财　马上还清！

刘　二　这……

莫海仁　这……这什么？还不起，是吗？把刘二带走，送官治罪！

三　姐　慢着，我哥哥犯了什么罪？

莫进财　你哥哥犯了什么罪？你犯罪了，你敢唱歌骂……

莫海仁　进财，休得啰唆，只要她答应亲事，就不用退田还债、送官治罪了。

三　姐　（唱）

说的什么媒？

提的什么亲？

明明起的是歪心。

葫芦里装的是什么药，

So many evictions fall on souls who have misery enough;

We are not alone, reduced to cutting firewood for a living.

Steward: You are certainly wasting my breath, Liu'er. Do you accept our offer or not?

Liu'er: Lord Mo will find one that more suits his taste than my sister, I reckon.

Lord Mo: I don't take any refusal on that account. Steward...

Steward (*producing his abacus and ledger*)**:** Last year you borrowed from us to see a doctor, Liu'er. The loan with compound interest comes to fifteen taels and twenty-seven cents. It is long outstanding. In sum, you have fallen behind in your payment.

Lord Mo: You must settle the accounts right away!

Steward: Yes. We must collect on the loan right away.

Liu'er: But...

Lord Mo: But... but what? You can't pay back and honor your word, is that it? How about stating your case in a court session in the Yamen?

Third Sister: Wait! What is my brother's crime?

Steward: His crime? You're the culprit. You perpetrate pouring a flow of invectives upon my lord with songs.

Lord Mo (*cutting him short*)**:** Hold your tongue, man. If she agrees to be my woman, her brother won't have to be evicted, liquidate the debt or be sent to the Yamen to be flogged.

Third Sister (*revolted*)**:**

What a match so mismatched from the outset!

What a marriage offer that abodes so ill!

It's plain you wish us evil.

I can see at one glance——

三姐一眼看得清。

　　　　众议论。

莫海仁　岂有此理，你竟敢说老爷是歪心！

三　姐　（唱）

　　　　霸山说是葬祖坟，

　　　　恨我你又来提亲，

　　　　外贴门神内有鬼，

　　　　分明怕我唱歌人。

　　　　众恍然大悟。

莫海仁　什么？老爷怕你唱歌？

莫进财　众位，老爷还会怕她唱歌？笑话，笑话。

三　姐　那好嘛!（唱）

　　　　三姐生来脾气怪，

　　　　只爱山歌不爱财，

　　　　你既不怕我唱歌，

　　　　结亲先要摆歌台，

　　　　谁能唱歌唱赢我，

　　　　不用花轿走路来。

莫海仁　什么，要对歌？

三　姐　按我们壮家的规矩，要想结亲就对歌！

莫进财、媒婆　老爷，这可不能答应呀！

What axes you have to grind!

(*The villagers start whispering together.*)

Lord Mo (*taken aback*): How dare you say I wish you evil? Consider again the gloomy prospect of being evicted.

Third Sister (*censoriously*):

To plunder a common property, he ostensibly claims back his ancestral graves;

To get rid of his true sorrow, which is me, he has proposed marrying me.

A double-dealer character acting out a weird plot,

He seems really apprehensive of my songs, not me.

(*The villagers begin to make sense of it.*)

Lord Mo (*in a huff*): Preposterous! You think I am scared of your songs?

Steward (*huffishly*): How could Mr. Mo be scared of her songs, good folk?

Third Sister: Very well, then. (*suddenly struck by a brilliant and bold idea*)

Your marriage proposal being so odd, much like my character.

Singing matters more than money in my estimation.

Here is my counter-proposal: marry me together with my songs.

I deem it most advisable to settle our dispute by holding a singing contest.

Should you or anyone of your hirelings outshine me,

I'll be your woman even forfeiting any dowry.

Lord Mo: You want a singing match, eh?

Third Sister: Our Zhuang custom is to arrange a singing match in which the wooer is put through his facings.

Steward and Matchmaker: Don't listen to her, sir!

莫海仁　我若有人唱得过你，你就嫁给我？

三　姐　有人？（想）若是唱不赢我呢？

莫海仁　这个……从此不提婚事。

三　姐　再不准霸占西山茶林！

莫海仁　这个嘛……

群　众　你不敢答应了吧？

莫海仁　好的！

三　姐　说话当真？

莫海仁　当真！

三　姐　不得反悔！

莫海仁　堂堂老爷，哪有反悔之理。

众　人　好！我们作证。

莫海仁　是！

　　　　莫海仁等下。

小　牛　三姐，对歌的时候我给你打鼓助威！

兰　芬　我把村里会唱歌的人都找来。

众　人　对！

　　　　——幕落

Lord Mo: If I hire someone, who can outsing you, you'll be my woman?

Third Sister: You'll hire someone? (*She thinks.*) Fine. Suits me down to the ground. What if he fails?

Lord Mo: Why... I'll drop the idea.

Third Sister: And recall your injunction?

Lord Mo: As for that...

Crowd: Don't you dare agree?

Lord Mo: All right, I agree.

Third Sister: You mean it?

Lord Mo: Certainly!

Third Sister: You won't go back on your word?

Lord Mo: How can a man of honor like me go back on his word?

Crowd: Very well. We're witnesses.

Lord Mo: Let's go.

    (*Lord Mo and his followers leave.*)

Xiaoniu: Third Sister, I'll beat the drum at the singing match to encourage you.

Lanfen: And I'll bring all the singers in the village to cheer you up.

Crowd: Splendid! (*The lights gradually dim.*)

    (*Curtain.*)

第五场　对歌

中幕前。

第四场的若干日后，莫进财率四家丁挑歌书书箱过场。

陶、李、罗三秀才上。老渔翁迎面上。

陶秀才 （唱）

　　桃花开放二月天，

李秀才 （接唱）

　　李花遍地白连连，

罗秀才 （接唱）

　　落花有意随流水，

老渔翁 （接唱）

　　狗屁不通臭上天。

陶秀才　老艄公，你讲什么？

老渔翁　我讲"天连水来水连天"。

陶秀才　小小一条河怎称得上"天连水来水连天"？

李秀才　真是不通之至也！

老渔翁　怎见不通？

李秀才　陶、李、罗是我等三人姓氏，你懂得吗？

老渔翁　你们讲的是头，我讲的是尾呀！

罗秀才　请道其详。

ACT FIVE
Singing Is Contesting and Believing

Time: A few days since the last scene.

Venue: In front of the inner curtain.

>(*The steward and four servants fetching cases of song books pass by. Enter three scholars, Tao, Li and Luo. The old fisherman comes in from the opposite side.*)

Tao: Peach blossoms under the spring sky.

Li: Plum's white petals on the ground are spread.

Luo: Fallen flowers float down the river.

Old Fisherman: Rot like this stinks.

Tao: What did you say, old man?

Old Fisherman: I said "The waters spread to meet the sky".

Tao: How can you say of such a small stream "The waters spread to meet the sky"?

Li: It does not make any sense.

Old Fisherman: How? Please elaborate.

Li: The words "peach", "plum" and "fallen" suggest our names, understand?

Old Fisherman: You are talking about the beginning of the lines, but I am referring to the end of your lines.

Luo: Pray elucidate.

老渔翁 你们的诗一个是天,一个是连,一个是水,是不是?

罗秀才 不错,不错。

老渔翁 我把你们三人的尾巴这样一抓,岂不是"天连水来水连天"吗?

陶秀才 妙哉!

李秀才 佳句!

罗秀才 佳句也!

陶秀才、李秀才、罗秀才 (同)

佳句也!

李秀才 二位仁兄,莫老爷不惜重金,请我等三人来此与刘三姐对歌,必须深思熟虑,不可信口开河。

陶秀才 李兄言之过矣!想我等皆一方名士,小小一土民村姑有何惧哉!

罗秀才 陶兄言之有理,不过小弟才疏学浅,此次冒上歌场,万一沙罐破底,则无地自容矣!

李秀才 罗兄,休长他人志气,灭自己威风。就凭我等随身所带之歌

Old Fisherman: Your lines end with respectively "sky", "spread" and "waters", don't they?

Luo: That is so.

Old Fisherman: So I poeticize by stringing the above three words to the effect "The waters spread to meet the sky".

Tao: Splendid word play!

Li: I concur with your opinion.

Luo: So do I.

Three Scholars: Yes, great minds think alike.

Li: Gentlemen, you are universally known and admired. The fact that Lord Mo has invited you to match Third Sister in singing is a proof of your prodigious talents in letters and singing. Make sure you team up to best that country maid to be worthy of his trust.

Tao: You are such an over-thinker, brother Li. We have worked hard at the classics. We have passed our studious boyhood and youth all the way. Now we are all too noted scholars in letters to be scared by a country maid. We have got the right training for such an occasion.

Luo: Brother Tao is right. We are received worthily. We must all thank him for the honor and consideration he has showed towards us. Yet, my strength is slight, and my talent, small. I must confess my relative inadequacy compared with you two. I have mustered the singular courage to be here. I pray my performance will be up to the level of yours so that I will not let Lord Mo down. Anyway, I am on standby in full battle array.

Li: Cheer up, my friend. Don't speak so highly of your fiend, brother Luo, or

书……

　　　　莫进财上。

莫进财　三位先生，船已备好。

陶秀才　歌书可曾装好？

莫进财　装了满满一船。

陶秀才、李秀才、罗秀才（同）

　　　　此次对歌必操胜券无疑矣！

老渔翁　上船啰！

　　　　陶、李、罗三秀才相让而下，老渔翁随下。

　　　　莫海仁上，媒婆、家丁、丫鬟随上。

莫海仁　进财！带上花轿，准备过江。

媒　婆　这个包在我身上，随后就到，请老爷放心。

莫进财　老爷今日对歌，必定马到成功。

媒　婆　马到成功！

莫海仁　哈哈哈，上船！

　　　　众下。

　　　　——中幕启

时　　　接过场。

景　　　河边一小山坡上，矗立着两株高大的木棉树，鲜红的花朵挂满
　　　　枝头，小牛在树下擂鼓助威，若干青年歌舞相伴。

　　　　人们在歌声中陆续上。

debase yourself. Besides, think of all the song books we have brought with us.

(*Enter the steward.*)

Steward: Gentlemen, the boat is ready.

Tao: Have you loaded the special cargo?

Steward: A whole boatload of songbooks.

Three Scholars: We are bound to prevail upon the country maid.

Old Fisherman: All aboard!

(*After much courtesy displayed to each other the three scholars board the boat followed by the old fisherman.*)

(*Enter Lord Mo with the matchmaker, servants and maids.*)

Lord Mo: Steward, make sure the bridal sedan-chair be ready with us. I will lose no time to cart off my bride.

Matchmaker: Yes, sir; rest easy on that count.

Steward: In the forthcoming pageant you must hasten the success. Make it a speedy job, and a landslide one as well.

Matchmaker: How well you have expressed the sentiments present!

Lord Mo: Aha! All aboard now.

(*All exit.*)

(*The inner curtain rises.*)

Time: Immediately after.

Venue: On a small hill by the river are two tall kapok trees with red blossoms on the boughs. Xiaoniu is drumming under the trees to encourage the contestants, while some young people are singing and dancing.

(*A crowd gathers.*)

众 人 （唱）

> 山对山，崖对崖，
>
> 河边搭起斗歌台；
>
> 一声歌起山河应，
>
> 不怕虎狼打队来。
>
> 山对山，崖对崖，
>
> 河边搭起斗歌台；
>
> 唱平江心三尺浪，
>
> 遮日乌云也唱开。
>
> 亚木跑上。

亚 木 小牛哥！听说今天来和三姐对歌的，是莫家特地从外地请来的秀才！

小 牛 莫说是从外地请来的秀才，就是京城请来的状元也不怕他。

> 三姐边唱边上，后随刘二、兰芬、韦老奶。

三 姐 （唱）

> 一把芝麻撒上天，
>
> 我有山歌万万千，
>
> 唱到京城打回转，
>
> 回来还唱十把年。
>
> 群众热忱地、关切地招呼三姐。
>
> 老渔翁上。

老渔翁 喂，乡亲们，莫海仁请来的三个秀才从那边上岸了。

刘 二 三妹，莫海仁请来的三个秀才必定是满腹文章，你要用心对才是。

小 牛 乡亲们，我们请他一试，看他们是秀才还是蠢材。（领唱，众和）

Crowd (*proclaiming*):

> Mountain beyond mountain, peak beyond peak,
>
> Here's a singing duel by the riverside starring our best songbird,
>
> To rival three hired singers with the rule hammered out:
>
> If she wins, our sister is still her own,
>
> If losing out, Lord Mo's woman.
>
> The hills and streams warm up with cheers and crowd.
>
> Let tigers or wolves come in packs to parade their wares!

(Yamu runs in.)

Yamu: Xiaoniu, I've heard that the Mo family has hired three pundits to vie with Third Sister today.

Xiaoniu: Either hired or invited, they are no match with our Third Sister!

(Enter Third Sister singing, followed by Liu'er, Lanfen and Grandma Wei.)

Third Sister (*with buoyance*):

> Like sesame seeds tossed into the sky,
>
> I have the richest repertoire of songs;
>
> How about singing with me all the way to the capital and back,
>
> And then for another ten years and more?

(The crowd gives Third Sister thunderous applauses.)

(Enter the old fisherman.)

Old Fisherman: Well, folks! The three scholars invited by Lord Mo are coming.

Liu'er: Sister, be careful. It will be very tough, I mean, the singing contest, with hired talents into the arena.

Xiaoniu: We will size them up, friends, to see whether they are scholars or

唱歌就唱两三排，

三头两句你莫来，

三头两句你莫唱，

快卷包袱穿草鞋。

歌声中陶、李、罗三秀才上场。

罗秀才 好大的口气。

陶秀才 莫老爷未到，我们可以置之不理。

李秀才 知己知彼，百战百胜，不妨见见刘三姐是何等人也。（问）你们
哪个是刘三姐？

老渔翁 （唱）

上山砍柴要用刀，

出门过河要架桥；

壮家用歌来问话，

无歌你就夹尾逃。

陶、李、罗三秀才茫然。

三　姐 （唱）

隔山唱歌山答应，

隔水唱歌水回声；

今日歌场初见面，

三位先生贵姓名？

陶秀才 问我等姓名？

陶、李、罗三秀才不直接道出姓名，各吟游一句。

陶秀才 （唱）

dunces. (*He leads off in a song and the others join in the crowd.*)

In singing, one must heed the code,

Which is to sing in the stanza in succession.

Be short of keeping to the agreed pattern,

And pack up at once and off you go.

(*The three scholars come in.*)

Luo: They are challenging us!

Tao: Since Mr. Mo isn't here yet, we might take a break first.

Li: Get to know yourself. Never overate your enemy. Such knowledge is vital in a war situation. So teaches us Sun Zi in his *Art of War*. Let's do some homework about the background info of our rival, the so-called... (*To the villagers*) Which of you is Third Sister?

Old Fisherman (*provoking*):

To cut wood in the hills you must bring along an axe;

To cross a river, you must turn to where there is abridge;

Our folk are accustomed to verbal exchanges by singing;

If you can't sing, you don't qualify for this contest!

(*The scholars are taken aback.*)

Third Sister (*with a naughty smile*):

Sing with me! The hills will respond.

Join me and the rivers will resound.

The singing contest draws rare singers.

For courtesy, your three exalted names?

Tao: She is asking our names.

(*Without replying directly, each declaims a line of verse.*)

Tao: I am first of the flowers of spring.

争春花开我最先，

李秀才 （接唱）兄红吾白两相连，

罗秀才 （接唱）报信敲来震天响，

陶秀才、李秀才、罗秀才 （同唱）

三人歌才赛歌仙。

三　姐　哦，你们三人一个姓陶，一个姓李，一个姓罗，对不对？（唱）

姓陶不见桃结果，

姓李不见李花开，

姓罗不见锣鼓响，

三个蠢材哪里来？

罗秀才 果然厉害。

陶秀才 待我回她一首，以显我等威风。

李秀才 陶兄言之有理。

陶秀才 你是刘三姐吗？

老渔翁 （指三姐）她是刘三妹，你们是不是要和她试一试？

罗秀才、李秀才 刘三妹？

韦老奶 你对不过刘三妹，就莫再找刘三姐啦，三姐比她还厉害！

陶秀才 先给她来个下马威！（唱）

牛角不尖不过界，

马尾不长不扫街，

我若不是画眉鸟，

怎敢飞往这里来。

三　姐　（唱）

Li: I follow my brother; he is red, I am white.

Luo: I shake the sky when I announce my news.

Three Scholars: Heaven has made us talents. We are not made in vain.

Third Sister: So one of you is named Tao, another Li and another Luo, is that

right? (*She sings.*)

You, Tao, you do not bear fruit;

You, Li, you do not blossom;

You, Luo, you make no sound——

What wind has blown these three idiots here?

Luo: We're up against it, all right!

Tao: Let's impress her by answering with a quatrain.

Li: Right, brother Tao.

Tao: Are you Third Sister?

Old Fisherman (*pointing to Third Sister*)**:** She's the younger daughter of the Liu

family. Do you want to try her out?

Luo and Li: The younger sister?

Grandma Wei: If you can't beat the younger sister, it's no use your looking for

Third Sister—— she's even stronger.

Tao: I'll give her a taste of what we can do. (*self-opinionated*)

A pointed ox horn tends to protrude at every turn.

A long broom of horse tail sweeps the floor clean.

But without musical prowess the equal of a thrush,

I would not step into the arena.

Third Sister (*undaunted*)**:**

你是山中画眉鸟，

我是游山打猎人，

利箭扣在弓弦上，

叫你有翅难飞行。

李秀才（唱）

没有真才我不来，

千里乘舟上歌台，

腹内藏着千万卷，

叫你呜呼又哀哉。

三　姐（唱）

书读万卷也白费，

你会腾云我会飞，

黄蜂歇在乌龟背，

你敢伸头我敢锥。

罗秀才（唱）

你莫恶来你莫恶，

你歌哪有我歌多，

不信你到船上看，

船头船尾都是歌。

三　姐（唱）

不懂唱歌你莫来，

看你也是无肚才，

唱歌从来心中出，

哪有船装水载来。

李秀才（唱）

小小黄雀才出窝，

You liken yourself to a singing thrush,

Quite unaware of a hunter stalking the prey.

With my arrow set on the bow,

I loosen it and you must regret.

Li (*screwing up his courage*):

Had I no talent I would not have come.

You are a real show-off, I can tell. You compare poorly with me,

As I have a hundred and eight thousand bushels of songs.

Soon you will regret for sure.

Third Sister (*tit for tat*):

How come? Somebody is bound to regret soon.

No matter how much you have read, If you glide, I can wing.

A wasp hovering above a tortoise head;

Dare you stick it out and I will sting.

Luo (*feeling slighted*):

Behold! That a country girl could be so profane.

I have more songs in stock than you can imagine.

See it for yourself and ape some humility.

For your reference, our boat is loaded with songbooks profusely.

Third Sister (*snapping back*):

Your singing deserves lousy rating!

Idle boast belies poor learning.

Songs come straight down from the bottom of the heart.

Would one call song a piece of cargo on boat?

Li (*bragging*):

A fledgling finch fresh from the nest, young and callow,

量你山歌也不多，

那日我从桥上过，

开口一唱歌成河。

三　姐　（唱）

你歌哪有我歌多，

我有十万八千箩，

只因那年涨大水，

五湖四海都是歌。

罗秀才　好厉害！

陶秀才　我来。（唱）

不知羞，

井底青蛙想出头，

见过几大天和地？

见过几多大河流？

三　姐　（唱）

住你口！

我是江心大石头，

经过几多风卷浪，

撞破几多大船头。

罗秀才　今日对歌，恐怕凶多吉少，不如及早趁风转舵。

陶秀才　尚未对歌，何出此不祥之言，罗兄真乃胆小如鼠也。

众　人　（唱）

对歌为何不还歌？

喉咙起了蜘蛛窝，

You ought not to have learned many songs, I surmise;

I'll tell you what, when I crossed the bridge the other day,

I raised my voice and lo! My songs flowed like a river.

Third Sister (*proudly*):

That's a funny boast, isn't it? You compare poorly with me,

For I have a hundred and eight thousand bushels of songs.

During the flood the other year,

My songs have broken loose, forming nine barrier lakes.

Luo: She really is sharp.

Tao: Let me try. (*insultingly*)

You have no sense of shame, given your rustic origin,

You bumpkin girl!

Be not a megalomaniac frog boasting at the bottom of a well!

How much of the world have you seen?

Third Sister (*retorting*):

Shut up!

Enough of all your pretension to intellect.

A boulder mid-stream, I have held out against too many torrents,

And capsized too many large vessels.

Luo: I'm afraid the prospect looks grim for us in this contest. I suggest we steer
clear while the wind holds fair.

Tao: How can you dampen our zest and eclipse our confidence before we've
even started? You are supposed to show more guts, brother Luo.

Crowd (*challenging*):

Why don't you respond to our sister?

Have spiders spun webs in your throats?

你既拜过孔夫子，

莫把歌场丢冷落。

此时有人喊，"莫海仁来了"。

莫海仁率莫进财、丫鬟、家丁上。

莫海仁 三位先生对赢了吧！来呀，接人。

陶秀才 且慢，方才我们和刘三妹试了几首，还未分胜负。

莫海仁 哪里有个刘三妹？

李秀才 那个不是？

莫进财 那就是刘三姐嘛！

罗秀才 明明讲是刘三妹嘛！

莫进财 刘三姐！

陶秀才、李秀才、罗秀才 刘三妹！

莫海仁 刘三姐哪里有妹妹！

春　姐 三妹！

陶秀才、李秀才、罗秀才 哎，哎！

冬　妹 三姐！

莫进财 哎，哎，哎！

罗秀才 喂，你到底是刘三妹呀还是刘三姐！

兰　芬 我们比她小的就叫她三姐，比她大的就叫她三妹，那你说她是
三姐还是三妹？

罗秀才 有理，有理！

李秀才 难怪，难怪。

陶秀才 原来如此。

众哄笑。

Since you claim to be scholars,

You mustn't let silence fall.

(*Someone calls out: "Mo Hairen is here!" Enter Lord Mo with his steward, maids and servants.*)

Lord Mo: I view this match a child's game. You gentlemen must have prevailed already. Come, cart off the bride to my estate!

Tao: Wait a minute! We have simply tried a few songs with the younger sister. The outcome is not yet announced.

Lord Mo: What younger sister?

Li: Isn't that the girl?

Steward: That is Third Sister.

Luo: But they told us clearly she was the younger sister.

Steward: No, Third Sister.

Three Scholars: No, the younger sister.

Lord Mo: Surely Third Sister does not have a younger sister.

Chunjie: Younger sister!

Three Scholars: You see!

Dongmei: Third Sister!

Steward: You see? You see?

Luo: Listen! Are you Third Sister or her younger sister?

Lanfen: Those younger than her call her Third Sister, those older call her "younger sister". What would you call her?

Luo: Quite right.

Li: No wonder.

Tao: So that's it.

(*The crowd breaks into with laughter.*)

莫海仁　三位先生赶快对来，对赢了重重有赏。

老渔翁　对歌了!

莫海仁　哪位先唱?

陶秀才　我先来!（唱）

　　　　之乎者也矣焉哉，

　　　　不读诗书哪有才!

　　　　开天辟地是哪个!

　　　　哪个把天补起来!

三　姐　（唱）

　　　　开口就是矣焉哉，

　　　　之乎者也烂秀才，

　　　　开天辟地是盘古，

　　　　女娲把天补起来。

李秀才　（唱）

　　　　出个谜子给你猜，

　　　　什么长年土中埋?

　　　　一旦出头惊天地，

　　　　谁不知我是高才。

三　姐　（唱）

　　　　你是竹笋在山间，

　　　　脸皮厚来嘴巴尖，

　　　　肚里空空无料子，

Lord Mo: Gentlemen, carry on with the match. If you win, I shall reward you well.

Old Fisherman: I proclaim the match begins.

Lord Mo: Who will start?

Tao: (*browbeating*)

Gross impertinence!

Such boorish manners only betray lowborn features and uncultured breeding.

One never knows how to conduct himself properly in society,

Unless at birth raised on the Confucian canon.

Answer me now, who created heaven and earth?

Who mended the vault of heaven?

Third Sister (*retorting*):

No more invoking sages of antiquity!

The more you do, the sillier you grow.

Pan Ku it was who made heaven and earth,

And Nu Wa who mended heaven.

Li (*softening his aggressive tone*):

Here is a riddle for you to solve:

What lies long buried in the ground,

Springing forth to astonish heaven and earth?

Who doesn't know the great height I attain?

Third Sister (*sharply*):

You are the bamboo-shoot in the hills,

Thick-skinned, with a beak-shaped tongue;

But empty and hollow inside,

只好挖来换臭钱。

罗秀才 （唱）

　　莫逞能，

　　三百条狗四下分，

　　一少三多要单数，

　　看你怎样分得清？

三　姐 （唱）

　　九十九条打猎去，

　　九十九条看羊来，

　　九十九条守门口，

　　还剩三条……

陶秀才、李秀才、罗秀才　呵！怎么样，三条什么？

三　姐 （唱）狗奴才。

　　众哄笑。

陶秀才 （唱）

　　你聪明，

　　一个大船几多钉？

　　一箩谷子几多颗？

　　问你石山有几斤？

三　姐 （唱）

　　是聪明，

　　大船数个不数钉，

　　谷子论斤不数颗，

　　你抬石山我来称。

　　陶、李、罗三秀才急忙翻书。

李秀才 （唱）

Dug up for a few coins.

Luo (*trying out her wits again*):

Stop boasting of your wit!

Divide three hundred dogs into four;

Each part an odd number, three large and one small——

Let's see what you make of that!

Third Sister (*tauntingly*):

Sell ninety-nine at the county fair,

Salt cure ninety-nine in your chamber;

And have ninety-nine watch your house,

This should leave you three at the rich men's beck and call.

Three Scholars: Well! What of them?

Third Sister (*explaining*): ...dogs as scurvy scholars.

(*The crowd roars with laughter.*)

Tao (*more riddle verses*):

Tell me, if you are sharp of wit.

How many nails a big boat has?

How many grains a bushel contains?

How many catties does the rocky mountain weigh?

Third Sister (*instantly*):

I can tell you this:

You count the boats, not the nails;

You reckon grain by weight not by number;

And if you'll bring me the mountain, I'll weigh it for you.

(*The three scholars rake among their song books.*)

Li (*singing*): What is round above and square below?

什么上圆下四方？

陶秀才 （唱）

什么下圆上四方？

罗秀才 （唱）

什么内圆方在外？

陶秀才、李秀才、罗秀才 （同唱）

什么外圆内四方？

三　姐 （唱）

箩筐上圆下四方，

筷子下圆上四方，

火盆内圆方在外，

铜钱外圆内四方。

陶、李、罗三秀才语塞，目瞪口呆，胡乱翻书。

罗秀才 这首，这首。

陶秀才 不好，不好，这首她对得出的。

莫海仁 快对，快对。

陶、李、罗三秀才仍无歌，众哄笑。

兰　芬 （唱，众和）

唱歌莫给歌声断，

吃酒莫给酒壶干，

既然敢来把歌对，

为何不见把歌还？

媒婆与家丁上。

媒　婆 花轿来迟了，花轿来迟了，新人快上轿吧！

Tao (*singing*): What is round below and square above?

Luo (*singing*): What is round within and square without?

All Three (*singing*): What is round without and square within?

Third Sister (*easily*):

> A crate is round above and square below;
>
> Chopsticks are round below and square above;
>
> Braziers are round within and square without;
>
> Copper coins are round without and square within.
>
> (*The scholars, much dismayed, do not know how to go on. They rummage among their volumes again.*)

Luo: This one, this one.

Tao: No good, no good. She can answer that.

Lord Mo: Hurry up!

> (*The scholars run out of songs. Another fit of laughter broken into from the crowd.*)

Lanfen (*provoking while the others join in*):

> In singing, there must be no pause;
>
> In drinking, the wine jug must stay filled.
>
> An empty jug can be refilled,
>
> But pause in a contest pronounces a dead loss on one party.
>
> (*Enter the matchmaker and the servants.*)

Matchmaker: Here comes the sedan-chair. Now let the bride get in quickly.

　　　　　接亲鼓乐由远而近，众人哄笑。

莫海仁　（狼狈地）先退下去，先退下去！

　　　　　媒婆退后，四家丁下。

莫海仁　（见势不对）今日三位先生远路而来，舟车劳累，对歌暂时到此
　　　　　而止，改日再分胜负。

小　牛　（唱，众和）

　　　　　山歌擂台已摆开，

　　　　　输赢未分怎下台？

　　　　　半路收场你认输，

　　　　　你不认输再唱来。

莫海仁　好，唱！

陶秀才　（唱）

　　　　　你莫狂，

　　　　　孔子面前卖文章，

　　　　　麻雀怎与凤凰比，

　　　　　种田哪比读书郎。

三　姐　（唱）

　　　　　真好笑，

　　　　　关公面前耍大刀，

　　　　　我们不把五谷种，

　　　　　要你饿得硬条条。

罗秀才　（唱）

　　　　　真粗鲁，

　　　　　皆因不读圣贤书，

(*Music for the wedding approaches. Thunderous uproar from the crowd.*)

Lord Mo (*embarrassed*): You lousy imbeciles. Keep away for the moment!

(*The matchmaker goes off followed by four servants.*)

Lord Mo (*seeing that things are going badly*): These three gentlemen have had quite a journey here. Let me call this a day for the moment and resume it some other day.

Xiaoniu (*challenging while the others join in*):

We are barely half way through the contest,

How can you quit before the outcome's out?

If you leave now, admit defeat first;

If you refuse to be a loser, you must roughen it out.

Lord Mo: Very well. Go on singing.

Tao (*bracing himself*):

Barbarity!

Peddling your learning before our patron saint Confucius?

A sparrow cannot compare with the royalty of phoenix.

Neither can a farmhand, with a scholar well versed in the Confucian canon!

Third Sister (*tauntingly*):

Ridiculous!

You make us all suffer fools gladly!

One thing is clear: if we stop growing wheat and corn,

You'll all starve to death, with your academic pretension.

Luo (*haughtily*):

What a bumpkin!

A good lesson to the unlettered class!

不读四书不知礼，

劝你先学人之初。

三　姐　（唱）

饭桶秀才死读书，

看你越读越糊涂，

不如跟我种田地，

帮拉犁耙种稻谷。

李秀才　（唱）

你发狂，

开口敢骂读书郎，

惹得圣人生了气，

从此天下无文章。

三　姐　（唱）

笑死人，

开口秀才最聪明，

问你几时种麦子？

问你几时种花生？

陶、李、罗三秀才目瞪口呆。

兰　芬　快答！快答！

陶秀才　（只好信口开河，唱）

你发昏来你发昏，

这点小事问我们，

阳春三月种麦子，

八月十五种花生。

众大笑。

韦老奶　（唱）

Proper manners for a lass come only,

When she is initiated into the sages' learning.

Third Sister:

Education proves your undoing.

The more you read, the dummier you are.

Far better turn a new leaf in life,

And be a farmer the rest of your lives.

Li (*brazening it out*):

Are you out of your mind,

That you even dare revile and insult scholars,

To such an extent that even our patron saint Confucius is implicated?

Such profanity only augurs an era of barbarism.

Third Sister (*continuing her taunts*):

You stuffy pedants!

Enough of your intellectual vainglory.

Answer me when we farmers grow wheat?

When do we grow peanuts?

(*Three scholars are dumb-confounded.*)

Lanfen: Answer the question, quick!

Tao (*making a bold guess*):

You must have lost your senses,

To ask about such trifles.

In the third month we sow wheat;

In the middle of the eighth month peanuts.

(*The crowd explodes with laughter.*)

Grandma Wei (*scornfully*):

笑死人，

哪有八月种花生？

若还三月种麦子，

要你狗屎吃不成。

三　姐　（唱）

秀才只会吃白米，

手脚几曾沾过泥，

一块大田交给你，

怎样耙来怎样犁？

陶、李、罗三秀才互相推让，陶、李将罗推出。

罗秀才　（唱）

听我言，

我家田地宽无边，

耙田犁地我试过，

牛走后来我走先。

众人更大笑不已，莫海仁气得讲不出话来。

李秀才　谁和你们讲犁田耕地，要讲……就讲天文地理。

三　姐　（唱）

A truce to folly!

The wrong season one sows peanuts in the eighth month!

If you sow wheat in the third month,

You will end up eating shit and horse dung.

Third Sister (*looking straight in their faces*):

It is a sad spectacle since the earth was born:

What all the rich men are well up to is idling and feasting,

Without ever bothering to have their hands and feet muddied at manual labor.

I wonder whether you know what to make of your bragging if I ask you:

What are the uses of four seasons?

What are the cycles of all farming?

If given a plot of land, how would you harrow?

How would you plough?

(*The scholars surge each other to answer. Tao and Li nudge Luo forward.*)

Luo (*forcing himself*):

A trifle query indeed. Hear me for what I know:

Since my family estate consists of hundreds of hectares of prime farmland,

And I did try my hand once at ploughing;

I kind of walked in front and while the ox plodded behind.

(*The villagers are convulsed in laughter. Lord Mo is rendered speechless.*)

Li: Let's sing a different song. Suppose we talk... er... of astronomy or geography.

Third Sister (*barely suppressing her contempt*):

你讲地来就讲地，

你讲天来就讲天，

天上为何有风雨？

地上为何有山川？

陶秀才 （无赖地）哪一个要和你们讲天比地，我们讲眼前。

三　姐 （唱）

讲眼前，

眼前眉毛几多根？

问你脸皮几多厚？

问你鼻梁几多斤？

陶、李、罗三秀才张口结舌，无歌可答，众人哄笑。

三　姐 （唱，众和）

风吹桃树桃花谢，

雨打李花李花落，

棒打烂锣锣更破，

花谢锣破怎唱歌？

莫海仁 快对呀！

罗秀才 （唱）

见你种田受奔波，

常年四季打赤脚，

不如嫁到莫家去，

穿金戴银住楼阁。

三　姐 （唱）

Astronomy or geography,

Talk of anything as you like.

What makes wind and rain in the sky?

What makes hills and streams on earth?

Tao (*boldfaced*):Who say we'd talk of heaven and earth? Let's discuss what's

right before your eyes.

Third Sister (*casually*):

As you please. Let's talk about things close by.

How many hairs do your eyebrows grow?

How thick is the skin of your face?

How heavy does your nose weigh?

(*The scholars are dumbfounded, unable to answer. The crowd bursts out with*

laughter again.)

Third Sister (*with finality while the crowd joins in*):

Everybody can tell your effort is lost.

Wind blows flowers all over the sky;

A sharp downpour batters flowers off their boughs;

Gongs and drums cannot withstand heavy beatings.

Peach, pear, drum, and gong, all are worn-out or done.

Lord Mo (*frantically*): Answer her quickly!

Luo (*tempting her*):

You are made above such a harsh living,

Barefoot fishing about and toiling away.

Why not be Lord Mo's woman,

One could be saved so much misery.

Third Sister (*giving him a thorough trouncing*):

三姐不怕受奔波，

你爱穿金住楼阁，

何不劝你亲妹子，

嫁到莫家做小婆？

莫进财 （唱）

莫家有势又有财，

丫鬟小子两边排。

媒　婆 （唱）

你若嫁到莫家去，

出门三步有人抬。

三　姐 （唱）

莫夸财主家豪富，

财主心肠比蛇毒，

塘边洗手鱼也死，

路过青山树也枯！

莫海仁 岂有此理！

陶秀才 你出口伤人！

三　姐 （接唱）

高高山上低低坡，

三姐爱唱不平歌，

再向秀才问一句，

为何富少穷人多？

陶秀才 （唱）

穷人多者不少也。

李秀才 （唱）

富人少者是不多。

How snobbish and rude of you to say so!

We are poor but decent people unlike you.

So glib of tongue, why not get your sister,

To be conjugal with that old rascal?

Steward (*plaguy*):

The Mo family has immense influence and wealth,

With pages and maids in rows in attendance.

Matchmaker (*smugly*):

If you marry into the Mo family,

You'll be for sure marrying the best Sugar Daddy.

Third Sister (*tauntingly*):

There you are, shameless eulogist of the moneyed.

Lackey to the viper!

He washes his hands in a pond and the fish die;

He passes the green hills and the trees wither.

Lord Mo (*disgruntled*): How dare you!

Tao: This is slander!

Third Sister (*jestingly*):

High the mountain, low the valley,

Third Sister loves to sing against injustice.

Let me ask these learned scholars:

Why are there so few rich men, so many poor?

Tao (*singing*): The poor are many, being not a few.

Li: The rich are few, not being many.

罗秀才 （唱）

  不少非多多非少。

莫海仁 （唱）

  快快回答莫啰唆。

  陶、李、罗三秀才手忙脚乱，乱翻歌书。

众　人 （唱）

  不会唱歌跟我来，

  帮我拿伞又拿鞋，

  拿伞拿鞋拿不动，

  丑死秀才去跳崖。

陶秀才、李秀才、罗秀才　告辞，告辞。

  陶、李、罗秀才狼狈下场。

老渔翁 （唱）

  回去啰，

  回去吃饭刮顶锅，

  一连吃它十把碗，

  免得到夜睡不着。

  众哄笑。

莫海仁 （念）

  你的山歌算什么，

  山歌怎比我家财多，

  舍得黄金三百两，

  要你有嘴难唱歌。

三　姐 （唱）

  知道你家钱财多，

  见着什么抢什么，

Luo: Not a few is not many, many is not few.

Lord Mo: Stop hedging and answer quickly!

(*The three scholars search frantically through their song books.*)

Crowd (*tauntingly*):

> Since we have carried the day and outsung you three,
>
> It seems you are left with only one option:
>
> Turn tail, flee home, practice singing one more decade,
>
> Before you are urged or hired to challenge me again.

Three Scholars: We'll take our leave.

(*They withdraw, thoroughly crestfallen.*)

Old Fisherman (*scoffing*):

> Fly, you, fly!
>
> Have a good bite all because of and despite the match lost.
>
> Make sure you are really well fed,
>
> That you would be guaranteed a good sleep tonight.

(*The crowd is thoroughly entertained.*)

Lord Mo (*petulantly*):

> How much does your singing amount to?
>
> By birth right I own a fabulous fortune.
>
> With whatever it takes of my gold,
>
> Your songs I will forever forbid.

Third Sister (*iconoclastically*):

> We know you are the richest lord,
>
> But the arch-villain in the neighborhood.

抢米粮，抢田地，
抢房屋，抢马骡，
假借风水霸茶山，
强抢民女做小婆，
只有嘴巴抢不去，
留着还要唱山歌！
众人复唱后四句。

莫海仁　你敢造反？

老渔翁　哈哈，莫大老爷，管他反也好，正也好，反正你是输了。

众　人（唱）
笑你癫来笑你疯，
灯草架桥枉费工，
桐油浇火火更旺，
竹篮打水一场空。
莫海仁气得发昏，退场。三姐对歌胜利，群众欢舞。

——幕落

You grab poor folk's grain,

You plunder their houses, horses, mules...

You seize our tea plantations,

Ostensibly for disturbing your ancestral graveyard,

You rob virgins and take other men's wives;

But my voice is one thing you can't rob,

My sympathy remains for the weak,

My vengeance, for the hateful established order.

(*The crowd joins in the last four lines.*)

Lord Mo (*astounded*): Is this a revolt?

Old Fisherman: Aha, Lord Mo, say what you like, you've been worsted in this contest.

Crowd (*in the spirit of defiance*):

Fume you may, chagrin as you like.

Waters keep rushing under a bridge;

Pour oil on flames, they burn the higher;

Collect water with a basket, you draw nothing home.

(*Exit Lord Mo bursting with fury. The villagers sing in triumph and dance for joy.*)

(*Curtain.*)

第六场　阴谋

时　　对歌后三五天。

景　　莫海仁家二堂。

中幕启，外面传来此起彼落的山歌声，莫海仁在室内不安地徘徊着。捧着金丝鸟笼的丫鬟随侍在侧。

山歌声　（唱）

唱山歌，

一人唱来万人和；

唱得穷人哈哈笑，

唱得财主打哆嗦。

莫海仁　（念）

可恼！可恼！真可恼！

山歌如烈火，把我烧。

这时山歌声大作。

莫海仁　（烦躁地）与我关起窗来！

丫鬟关窗，仍有山歌声。

莫海仁　（愤怒地）关门！

（把头蜷伏在太师椅上。）

丫鬟关门，仍有山歌声，莫海仁四处寻找，突然发现是笼中的鹩哥学唱，他勃然发怒。

莫海仁　（念）

小小畜生太猖狂，太猖狂。

你也唱歌把我伤，把我伤。（一把抓出笼中鹩哥）

ACT SIX
Lord Mo Is in League with the Magistrate

Time: Three or four days after the singing contest.

Venue: Lord Mo's inner chamber.

(As the inner curtain rises, folk songs are distinctly heard outside. Mo paces his room uneasily. A maid is in attendance with the bird cage.)

Crowd (*vociferously off-stage*):

Let us sing loud and out strong;

With open mouths our strong melodious songs.

We sing till the poor rejoice from their hearts,

Till the wicked tremble with fear.

Lord Mo (*irritated*):

Confound them, confound them!

These bastards drive me crazy!

(The singing grows louder.)

Lord Mo (*on tenterhooks*): Shut the windows!

(The maid shuts the windows, but still the singing can be heard.)

Lord Mo (*furiously*): Shut the door!

(He shrinks back in his chair.)

(The maid shuts the door, but still singing has not been hushed down. Lord Mo peers around and discovers that the parrot in the cage has been mimicking the singing outside. He flies into a fit of rage.)

Lord Mo (*with a grisly laugh*):

Heinous creature, you are, too, dare devil,

To sing out against me!

居然你也把反歌唱。

我要你一命见阎王、见阎王！

莫海仁狠狠地把鹩哥摔死，捧鸟笼的侍女惊叫了一声，莫海仁将她一脚踢开。

莫海仁　刘三姐，刘三姐，你叫我好恼，你叫我好恨！（唱）

实指望用巧计把她笼中关定，

谁料想闹得我狼藉坏了声名。

莫进财　（上，唱）

大集镇小峒场歌声如雷震，

莫进财急忙忙报与老爷听。

开门呵！（莫海仁开门，莫进财入室内）启禀老爷，外面成群结队的穷鬼四面八方而来，都要在今晚歌圩上会刘三姐，他们一边走一边唱……

莫海仁　唱些什么？

莫进财　还不是刘三姐的反歌。

莫海仁　这还了得！来呀！（四家丁各执匕首上）将刘三姐杀了，除掉这个祸根。

莫进财　不可，老爷当初说过，刘三姐深得人心，远近闻名。如今更是名扬千里，和那帮穷鬼鱼水不分，若是杀了她，定会造成大祸。

莫海仁　难道由她造反不成？

(*He pulls the parrot out of its cage.*)

Because you've sung the rebels' song,

You are doomed and damned!

(*He dashes the bird to the ground with a force, killing it. The maid holding the cage gives a cry of fear. Lord Mo kicks her aside.*)

Lord Mo (*flaring up*): You are to blame, Third Sister! I am really pissed off! (*To himself*)

I schemed to lock her in a cage,

Instead of which my name was dragged in mud.

(*Enter the steward.*)

Steward (*his voice trembling*):

Songs are pressing hard on our hearts like thunders.

I hasten to report this to my master.

May I come in? (*Lord Mo opens the door and the steward enters.*) I beg to report, sir, these hooligans are thronging in from all sides. Looks like a carnival is around the corner tonight. The energy is palpable throughout the entire district. Everybody is in the mood of partying out.

Lord Mo (*impatiently*): What are they singing?

Steward: What else but Third Sister's subversive stuff.

Lord Mo (*enraged*): Sedition! Sedition! Here! (*Enter four servants with daggers.*) I'll have Third Sister killed once and for all.

Steward: Master, let us not do anything rash, as you said yourself, sir, Third Sister is popular and well known. They enjoy her great popularity. She becomes their hope. Killing her would backfire.

Lord Mo: What! Shall we let her get away with this sort of mutiny?

莫进财　老爷何不奉上五百两纹银，另外修书一封，呈请州官下令禁歌。

　　　　　丫鬟正端茶上。

莫海仁　禁歌？

莫进财　刘三姐为首聚众，教唱反歌，煽惑刁民，辱骂老爷，当然要禁。

莫海仁　嘿嘿！倘若那丫头敢违抗禁令，如何是好？

莫进财　老爷，我们正好借此——（做一个抓人的手势）

莫海仁　好，纸、笔伺候。

　　　　　丫鬟下。

莫进财　正是。（念）牢笼巧计安排定，

莫海仁　（念）一心扰除眼中钉。

　　　　　丫鬟捧笔砚上，莫进财接过去。

莫进财　将帷幕放下！

丫　鬟　（放帷帐，偷听）待我快去告诉三姐。（下。）

　　　　——中幕落

Steward (*guilefully*): Why don't you bring the magistrate into the game, sir? A piddling amount of silver as his reward. What cat does not like fish? We will secure an official ban on all singing.

(*A maid comes in with tea.*)

Lord Mo: Forbid all singing?

Steward (*pandering to him*): Third Sister is the wire-puller behind the scene. She rallies the mob around her, ostensibly giving some music lessons. Such spiritually malevolent songs she teaches contain abusive language, expressions of social satire, mockery of authorities and even covert exhortations to rebellion. Every day I wail at such a general deplorable reversal of everyday rules and norms to our community. The social effects, I am afraid, would be disastrous had we not forestalled them.

Lord Mo: Hmm. What if the slut ignores it?

Steward: Why, that will allow us the heavy-handed option, doesn't it, sir? (*He makes the motion of arresting someone.*)

Lord Mo: Good, Bring paper and brush.

(*Exit the maid.*)

Steward: She is damned for sure this time.

Lord Mo: Come what may, I must pluck out this thorn in my flesh.

(*The maid brings in a brush and ink stone which the steward takes.*)

Steward: Put down the curtain.

(*The maid obeys as instructed and eavesdrops on their conversation, furtively tiptoeing out.*)

Maid: I must relay this vital message to Third Sister at once! (*Exit.*)

(*Curtain.*)

第七场　抗禁

中幕前，男女青年三五成群，穿着节日的服装，口唱山歌过场。

众　人　（唱）

　　唱山歌，

　　一人唱来万人和；

　　唱得穷人哈哈笑，

　　唱得财主打哆嗦。

　　兰芬、冬妹、韦老奶、小牛、亚木、老渔翁、三姐在歌声中陆

　　续上场。

冬　妹　听说今晚赶歌节的人好多呀！有翻山越岭来的，有撑船渡河来

　　的，今晚一定很热闹。

兰　芬　快走，快走，今晚歌圩上我一定要唱个痛快！

韦老奶　哪个要听你唱？人家都是来会刘三姐的啦。

　　众笑。

　　刘二背着锄头上。

刘　二　外婆，你们讲什么？

亚　木　二哥，今晚歌圩上有成千上万外乡来的人，找你家三姐学歌来

　　了，还说要请三姐到各地去传歌呢！

ACT SEVEN
Magistrate and Mo Are Foiled in Their Attempt

(*In front of the inner curtain there is a party fever that never stops. Here you will find a large crowd milling about, dressed in their season's best.*)

Crowd (*rejoicing*):

Let us sing loud and out strong;

With open mouths our strong melodious songs.

We sing till the poor rejoice from their hearts,

Till the wicked tremble with fear.

(*During the singing in come Lanfen, Dongmei, Grandma Wei, Xiaoniu, Yamu, the old fisherman and Third Sister.*)

Dongmei (*excitingly*): I've heard that this year's singing contest draws droves of enthusiasts and visitors in all directions, on foot, by boat, by thousands, as we have never seen or known. As we speak, they keep swarming to our place to get the most of a visit to see our dear Third Sister. She has been such a magnet.

Lanfen: Hurry up! We can't wait to sing to our hearts' content.

Grandma Wei: Show a bit of modesty. Everybody is here to hear the legend with their own ears!

(*The crowd laughs.*)

(*Enter Liu'er with his hoe.*)

Liu'er: Granny, what have you been talking about?

Yamu (*elated*): Liu'er, this evening thousands of folk near and far are congregating on the fixed location. The crowd seems gathering more and more people along the way, all for a look at Third Sister and

老渔翁　老二呀！你有这样好的一个妹子，该高兴了吧！走！到歌圩上你也得唱个痛快。

刘　二　老伯，我……我唱不好。

兰　芬　二哥，你不是还教我们唱过。（唱）

　　　　唱首山歌解心忧，

　　　　喝口凉水浇心头；

　　　　凉水……（装作忘记下面的歌词。）

刘　二　（接唱）

　　　　凉水解得心头火，

　　　　唱歌解得万般愁。

　　　　众笑，突然幕后有人喊："三姐！"众人止住笑声，莫家一丫鬟跑上。

丫　鬟　三姐！

三　姐　你是哪家姐姐？找我做什么？

丫　鬟　我是莫家的丫鬟。三姐，快回去吧！今晚千万不要赶歌圩了。

众　人　什么事？

丫　鬟　莫老爷说三姐唱了反歌，他已禀报官府，今晚就要派人前来禁歌，看样子……

众　人　怎么样？

丫　鬟　看样子是要抓三姐！

witness the event of her premiere show. Some even urge her to go back with them to spread her songs.

Old Fisherman: Liu'er, you have such an adorable sister and you make us all envious. Come, you must join us and sing a little bit to have your recent frustrations vented some way.

Liu'er: Uncle, I... I am not a good singer.

Lanfen: Why, cousin, didn't you teach us before? (*teasing him*)

I sing a song to drive away my sorrow,

I drink cold water to quench my thirst;

Cold water... (*she pretends to have forgotten the rest.*)

Liu'er (*continuing the song*):

Cold water can cool my fiery heart,

Songs can dissolve all my troubles.

(*The crowd cracks up. Suddenly someone off-stage calls: "Third Sister!" They stop laughing. Lord Mo's maid runs in.*)

Maid: Third Sister!

Third Sister: Who are you, sister? What can I do for you?

Maid (*in an undertone*): I am a maid in the Mo family. Third Sister, you must quit and leave! Beware of Lord Mo who attempts your life tonight.

Crowd: Why, what has happened?

Maid (*continuing in great agitation*): Mr. Mo has demonized your singing and reported on you to the magistrate that you have stirred up all the trouble. They will send soldiers to disrupt the event and to put you in prison.

Crowd: What?

Maid: They scheme to take Third Sister prisoner!

众沉寂片刻。

丫　鬟　三姐，我得赶快回去了。

三　姐　好，谢谢你了。

　　　　丫鬟下。

刘　二　三妹……怎么办呀？

老渔翁　哼！老狗斗歌斗不过，搬来官家……

小　牛　他敢碰一碰三姐，我们大家就跟他拼了！

兰　芬　对，他禁他的，我们唱我们的。走……

众　人　走！

三　姐　慢着，兰芬、冬妹，你们先去歌圩上，我们随后就来。二哥、老伯、
　　　　小牛，我们来商量一下。

　　　　众人围拢三姐，三姐布置歌阵。

小　牛　好！

老渔翁　哈哈哈！

　　　　灭灯。

　　　　——中幕启

时　　　第六场的当天晚上。

景　　　一轮明月高挂天空，月亮透过茂密的榕树<u>丛</u>林，照着远处山坡
　　　　上的花草。
　　　　三三五五的人群唱着山歌，在山林中漫步，有些人好像在盼望
　　　　和等待着什么，又有些人在互相询问和奔走相告。

(The crowd falls silent.)

Maid: I must go back now, Third Sister.

Third Sister: All right. Thank you.

(The maid leaves.)

Liu'er (*nervously*): Sister... what shall we do?

Old Fisherman (*gazing tensely at Third Sister*): Hmm. Because that old dog couldn't beat us in singing, he's brought in soldiers and magistrate now to ride roughshod on us. We have come to a pretty sorry pass.

Xiaoniu (*chiming in*): We must pull our heads together preparing for the worst. We must do everything to ensure our Sister is safe and sound.

Lanfen (*heatedly*): Yes, we must. Meanwhile, we will not balk down at that notion and we'll proceed with our festivity.

Crowd: Come on!

Third Sister (*fully assured*): Wait! Lanfen and Dongmei, you go ahead to the singing ground. We'll join you presently. Brother, uncle and Xiaoniu, come, we must talk.

(The crowd gathers around Third Sister while she unveils her emergence plan.)

Xiaoniu: Good!

Old Fisherman: Haha!

(The light grows dim.)

(The inner curtain rises.)

Time: Later that evening.

Venue: The singing ground.

(The moonlight beams through the thick foliage of the banyan trees onto the ground. The verdant hills and the scenic landscape make up for a delicious eye-

众　人（唱）

年年三月是歌节，

月儿明亮歌儿甜，

今年来了刘三姐，

歌声唱得月更圆。

音乐过门中，拿包袱、雨伞的一男一女外乡人询问本乡人。

外乡人甲　三姐还没有来？

外乡人乙　三姐呢？

外乡人甲　三姐怎么还不来呀？

本乡人甲　不晓得呀！

本乡人乙　等一等嘛！

本乡人甲　三姐就来啦！

众　人（唱）

一心想会刘三姐，

八方歌手四路来。

四处歌手都来到，

只等三姐上歌台。

兰芬、冬妹、春姐（边上边唱）

candy. Participants and spectators are milling about in the woods, awaiting the forthcoming show. One can feel the resonance of the drums, gongs and lutes echo through the village and brim over to the surrounding areas.)

Crowd (*blithely*):

> March is the merriest month in all the year,
>
> Whereupon our singing carnival does fall;
>
> Bright shines the moon amid sweet tunes;
>
> The waxing moon appears fuller and rounder.
>
> This year, with Third Sister here,
>
> Rejoiced such good tidings to hear,
>
> The poor folk flock from far and near.
>
> (*During the interlude a man and a woman from distant land, who have brought baggage and an umbrella, makes inquiries to locals.*)

First Stranger: Isn't Third Sister here yet?

Second Stranger: Where is she?

First Stranger: Why hasn't she shown up yet?

First Villager: No idea.

Second Villager: You'd better wait.

First Villager: I surmise she is around soon.

Crowd (*in the mood of festivity*):

> Eager to see Third Sister the legend in person,
>
> By thousands they come, by myriads and more;
>
> Such numbers have never been heard before,
>
> Awaiting for her to mount the platform.
>
> (*Enter Lanfen, Dongmei and Chunjie, singing.*)

Three Girls (*overwhelmed with a sense of pride*):

唱一声，

多谢四方众乡亲，

姐换新妆还未到，

我代三姐谢亲人。

兰　芬　乡亲们，三姐等下就来。

外乡人　三姐能来吗？

兰　芬　能来。

外乡人　三姐能来就好，我们从各地赶来就是为了拜会三姐，想请三姐
　　　　到我们那里去传歌。

其他外乡人也纷纷说"我也是来拜会三姐的"，兰芬、冬妹又和
他们小声说些什么，下场。

几个男女青年唱起情歌来。

男青年　（唱）

想妹一天又一天，

想妹一年又一年，

铜打肝肠都想断，

铁打眼睛也望穿。

女青年　（唱）

水泻滩头哗哗响，

妹不见哥心就忧，

喝茶连杯吞下肚，

千年不烂记心头。

男青年　（唱）

妹相思，

妹有真心哥也知，

The sons and daughters of the Zhuang are born singers,

Quite adept at the art of improvising songs as occasion requires.

And the moment for the most talented by far in the land,

To perform for us well-nigh draws near.

Lanfen: Third Sister will be here presently, friends and neighbors.

Stranger: She is on the scene, then?

Lanfen: Yes, she is amidst us.

Stranger: Lovely! Third Sister is certainly worth waiting for, despite the long and arduous journey. To witness how she will prove to rise above all the rest of singers.

(*Still, other strangers declare: "We come just to see our finest songbird." Lanfen and Dongmei whisper to them before going out.*)

(*Some young men and girls start courtship by singing love songs.*)

Young Man (*amorously*):

I yearn for my lass day after day,

Life has grown dullest without her nearby.

Even a heart of bronze would break with such tormenting desire;

Even eyes of iron would wear out with watching.

Girl (*echoing his avidity*):

The more you are out of sight, the more, on my mind.

My distraction is such that I drink tea together with all its dregs.

You are in my heart for a thousand years.

Young Man (*teasingly*):

Boys are so silly,

That they can never tell how much we love them.

蜘蛛结网三江口，

水冲不断是真丝（思）。

女青年 （唱）

哥相思，

哥有真心妹也知，

十字街头卖莲藕，

节节空心都是丝（思）。

男青年 唔喂！

女青年不好意思地跑开，壮族人民喜爱的绣球舞开始了。

女青年 （唱）

金丝绣球鲜又鲜，

千针万线妹手连，

绣球飞过相思树，

妹心落在哥身边。

男青年 （唱）

金丝绣球鲜又鲜，

千针万线妹手连，

哥接绣球胸前挂，

条条线把哥心牵。

这时莫进财与一家丁上。

莫进财 "哥接绣球胸前挂，条条线把妹心牵"，好，好歌！乡亲们，你
们要唱歌，就要唱这种歌，莫学刘三姐唱那种歪风邪气的怪歌。

So strenuous and sophisticated a work,

Of a spider weaving a web across a turbulent river.

Girl (*returning his jibes*):

That does not ring true.

Girls could be equally silly.

You see lotus root sold at the country fair,

The symbol of our love. Not as hollow as you believe.

Young Man: Ah, ha!

(*The girl, embarrassed, retires. The Embroidered Ball Dance, popular among the Zhuang people, begins.*)

Girl (*announcing*):

Bright the embroidered ball sewn with golden thread;

A thousand stitches I have sewed with my own hand;

I toss it over the tree of love;

Don't let it fall to the ground, my love.

Young Man (*equally love-sicken*):

The embroidered ball is such a token of love,

Sewn with threads as if drawn from your heart.

How could I fail to catch it?

Lo! It bangs right at my breast and every thread tugs at my heart.

(*Enter the Steward with servant.*)

Steward (*pontificating*): "How could I fail to catch it? Lo! It bangs right at my breast and every thread tugs at my heart." Good song. Far better than those spiritually polluted stuff. Fellow countrymen, here is a model melody everybody should emulate and hum. Our singing contest has more to offer than those risqué tunes or improper music by restive

老渔翁　莫管家，什么是歪风邪气的怪歌呀？

莫进财　那些骂财主的，不怕王法的，冒犯神灵的，都是歪风邪气的怪歌。

老渔翁　莫管家，你这一讲我倒糊涂了，我唱一首你听是好是坏！（唱）

　　　　什么大大四四方？

　　　　什么双双坐中堂？

　　　　什么样人常来往？

　　　　什么饱吞万担粮？

兰芬、冬妹　（唱）

　　　　猪栏大大四四方，

　　　　老爷奶奶……

老渔翁　（截唱）公猪母猪坐中堂。

兰芬、冬妹　（唱）

　　　　抢吃猪潲常来往，

　　　　饱吞千家万担粮。

老渔翁　莫管家，如何？

莫进财　唱一唱猪嘛倒还可以。

　　　　众笑。

老渔翁　（唱）

　　　　什么生来耳朵宽？

Third Sister.

Old Fisherman: What do you mean by risqué tunes, steward?

Steward (*pontificating further*)**:** Third Sister has pushed our rule to the limit. Most of her songs are admittedly beautiful and very appealing. However, their beauty and appeal disguise the content of the lyrics, which can be dark, profane and demonic. You must all take heed.

Old Fisherman (*pretending not to understand*)**:** Why, steward, the more you explain, the more confused I have grown. Let me sing you a song and you tell me whether it's proper or improper. (*in jest*)

What is roomy and square?

What couple sits there?

What kind of creatures trot to and fro?

What devours whole fans of grain?

Lanfen and Dongmei (*singing*)**:**

The pigsty is roomy and square,

The landlord and his wife...

Old Fisherman (*interrupting them to sing*)**:**

The bog and the sow sit there.

Lanfen and Dongmei:

They trot to and fro to grab food,

And devour whole tons of grain from countless homes.

Old Fisherman: How about that, steward?

Steward (*delighted*)**:** Pigs make perfect themes for singing.

(*The crowd laughs.*)

Old Fisherman (*riddle verse*)**:**

Who is born with big ears, robed in black and white with brocade

黑白花袍身上穿？

为何生来肚子大？

手脚不分背朝天？

韦老奶 （唱）

老爷生来耳朵宽，

黑白花袍身上穿，

老爷享福肚子大，

拜见皇帝背朝天。

莫进财 这倒是一首赞扬老爷福大命大的好歌。

众哄笑。

家　丁 莫管家，耳朵宽，肚子大，背朝天的是猪呀！

众大笑。

莫进财 （恼羞成怒）你等好大胆，竟敢……

老渔翁 莫管家，请你莫生气，这里还有一首好听的呢。（唱）

什么心肠比蛇毒？

什么跷脚等禾熟？

什么人是众人仔？

哪个聪明快答出。

兰芬、冬妹等 （唱）

财主心肠比蛇毒，

老爷跷脚等禾熟，

光吃不做众人仔，

千家养他享清福。

embroidery?

Who is born with a potbelly, legs and feet folded together?

Crawling on all fours, with back hunched against the sky?

Grandma Wei (*in jest*):

Lord Mo has massive ears as few do,

He is donning a black and white brocade gown.

And he will bend his head low,

Hunched back against the sky to hail the emperor.

Steward (*nodding in assent*): Praiseworthy. As it has extolled the virtues of my lord and wish all the best for Lord Mo.

(*The crowd roars with laughter.*)

Servant (*making sense of the riddle verses at last*): Why, steward, they are reviling our master, I am afraid, you see their riddle verse likens our lord to a pig growing big ears, a fat belly and its back in the air.

(*The crowd laughs.*)

Steward (*crossly*): The insolence! How dare you...

Old Fisherman: Calm down, steward. Here's a pleasant song. (*mockingly*)

Whose hearts turn out more venomous than those of vipers?

Who are laid back onto armchairs reaping what they haven't sowed?

Where do we turn to identify parasites among men?

Let whoever's sharp answer quickly!

Lanfen and Dongmei (*censoriously*):

The rich have hearts more venomous than a viper,

They are laid back onto armchairs till the crops are ripe;

They eat and idle, parasites among men;

Without our labors and contributions, they are set at naught.

莫进财　哎，哎，这就是刘三姐的歌。

兰　芬　我学会了就是我的歌。

众　人　我们学会了就是我们的歌。

莫进财　这是反歌，你们不要受刘三姐的挑唆。

亚木、亚祥等　（唱）

　　　　　如今世道荒唐多，

　　　　　水牛生蛋马生角，

　　　　　心有不平嘴要唱，

　　　　　哪用旁人来挑唆。

莫进财　众位乡亲，你们千万莫上刘三姐的当，唱了反歌是要杀头的呀。
　　　　莫老爷不让大家唱这种歌，是为了大家好哇……

老渔翁　（唱）

　　　　　如今世道颠倒颠，

　　　　　野猫给鸡来拜年，

　　　　　龙角生在猪头上，

　　　　　象牙长在狗嘴边。

莫进财　（一把抓住老渔翁）你这老鬼，不要在我面前装疯卖癫。刘三姐
　　　　就是你用船把她接来的。

　　　　莫海仁带四家丁上。

Steward (*feeling hoodwinked*): Ah, there you go, risqué stuff learned from Third Sister.

Lanfen: Since I've learned it, it's become mine.

Crowd: We've learned it, so it's our song.

Steward (*obviously annoyed*): Too racy for you. I advise you all turn back upon such subversive songs. You mustn't let Third Sister contaminate your souls.

Yamu and Yaxiang (*caustically*):

Weird things are now common occurrences,

As to behold horses grow horns and buffaloes lay eggs;

So much evil presses hard on the heart,

We sing without being incited up.

Steward (*with menacing voice and eyes*): Don't let Third Sister hoodwink you, fellow countrymen. Singing subversive songs are punishable by the law. It's for your own good that Mr. Mo has gone to great length to secure an official injunction on this year's singing festive season and suspend all subsequent celebrations.

Old Fisherman (*gazing distastefully into steward's face*):

Topsy-turvy the world has turned!

A weasel greets chicken happy New Year,

Dragon's antlers protrude from a swine's brow,

Ivories grow long from underneath beside the lips of a cur.

Steward (*rounding on the fisherman with a sudden viciousness*): You old scoundrel! Feigning ignorance, you actually know more than you reveal. It was you who sought them out from nowhere from the outset.

(*Enter Lord Mo with four servants.*)

莫海仁　住手！（在人群中寻找刘三姐。）

莫进财　老爷，刘三姐还没有来。

　　　　　三姐、小牛、刘二上场，随即隐没在群众中。

莫海仁　众位乡亲听了，刘三姐为首聚众，教唱反歌，今有州官传谕禁唱山歌。老爷我念她是外地来人，年幼无知，在州官面前与她担待，今后她须改邪归正，不许再唱山歌。

三　姐　（唱）

　　　　　州官出门打大锣，

　　　　　和尚出门念弥陀，

　　　　　皇帝早朝要唱礼，

　　　　　种田辛苦要唱歌。

莫海仁　刘三姐，你来了！

三　姐　听说州官传谕要拿我治罪，多蒙老爷担待，特来道谢。

莫海仁　刘三姐，只要你当众认错，不再唱山歌，老爷不但保你无罪，还重重有赏。

Lord Mo: Stop! (*He scouts Third Sister in the crowd.*)

Steward: Third Sister isn't here yet, sir.

(*Enter Third Sister, Xiaoniu and Liu'er to quickly mingle with the crowd.*)

Lord Mo (*with icy severity*): Listen, folk! This assemblage tonight has been infiltrated by pertly and unruly elements for socially disruptive purposes. Fugitives like Third Sister have landed within our jurisdiction and has bewitched our good compatriots with her angelic voice. Yet, her lyrics contain harmful anti-social content of whose consequences we must forestall. To the great benefit of our community, our beloved and wise magistrate has put a ban on singing as of today. Third Sister must rectify and expiate her misdeed. Any future transgressions will not be pardoned.

Third Sister (*protesting*):

Gongs are sounded when magistrates set out on a tour;

Monks chant a prayer while walking out;

Every courtier hails the emperor holding a morning court.

To enjoy our lighter moment, we sing out.

Lord Mo: So you are here, Third Sister.

Third Sister (*seemingly bewildered*): I hear that the magistrate has ordered my arrest, but that you have put in a word for me. I've emerged specially to thank you.

Lord Mo (*patronizingly*): If you realize how far you have gone astray and recognize your faults, Third Sister, I may pardon you and make you a role model of the prodigal girl who repents her misdeed of running others and getting them excited with pure slanders against benevolent squires like me.

三　姐　莫老爷，我年幼无知，不知错在何处，罪在哪里？

莫海仁　你聚众唱歌。

三　姐　什么叫聚众？

莫海仁　三人为众。

三　姐　聚众唱歌，该定何罪！

莫海仁　轻者责打，重者关监。

三　姐　那聚众为首的呢？

莫海仁　斩！

三　姐　众位乡亲，可曾记得我与莫海仁对歌之事？

众　人　记得！

三　姐　他请来了陶、李、罗三个秀才，不多不少正好三个。莫海仁，
　　　　聚众为首的是你，看来你的人头难保。

　　　　众人兴奋，纷纷道好。

莫海仁　（冷笑）刘三姐，你看这是什么？

莫进财　州官大令，禁唱山歌！（念）
　　　　土民不服王化，
　　　　唱歌扰乱民心，

Third Sister (*glowering at him*): Your people characterize me as pertly and unruly, Lord Mo, I am afraid they are twisting things up and fling baseless accusations. Would you be more specific?

Lord Mo (*smiling ominously*): To begin with, you have started a big band.

Third Sister (*feigning disbelief*): What's meant by a "big band"?

Lord Mo: Two people are company, three make a band.

Third Sister (*disbelieving him*): Jabberwocky! Gathering a singing band? Is there such a crime and even a law applicable to it? Enlighten me.

Lord Mo (*with a puzzled frown, insistently*): There is, for sure. First offenders will be beaten. As for more serious cases, I mean where repeated disciplinary action does not work, she or he will be put in jail.

Third Sister (*she looks at him with a sneer*): How about the wire-puller?

Lord Mo (*categorically*): Decapitation!

Third Sister (*challenging Lord Mo*): Fellow countrymen, do you all remember my singing contest with Mo Hairen?

Crowd: We do!

Third Sister (*gimlet-eyed*): He invited the three scholars Tao, Li and Luo. No more and no less, just three. So, Mo Hairen, as the ring-leader who has assembled a crowd, it seems you have already committed the crime you have named. Are you truly remorseful?

(*The excited congregation shouts approval.*)

Lord Mo (*irritated but with a malignant laugh*): Third Sister, do you see this?

(*His servant unrolls the magistrate's prohibition.*)

Steward: Here is the magistrate's order forbidding singing. (*proclaiming*)
The present magistrate announces that in view of the reports from good citizens lately of some unruly and obdurate elements taking

州官为民着想，

唱歌从此严禁。

三　姐　（唱）

天上大星管小星，

地上狮子管麒麟，

皇帝管得大官动，

哪个敢管唱歌人？

众和最后二句。

三　姐　乡亲们，我们还是唱歌去！

莫海仁　你敢！

众　人　唱歌去！

三　姐　走，我们唱歌去。

莫海仁　你敢唱！

三　姐　（唱）

山歌不唱忧愁多，

众　人　（唱）

大路不走草成窝，

铜刀不磨生黄锈，

胸膛不挺背要驼。

莫进财带家丁追下。

莫海仁　乡亲们……

众　人　（唱）

refuge within my jurisdiction and teaching subversive songs to sow seeds of rebellion amongst the populace, such acts are tantamount to the crime of treason, thus subject to the full penalty of the law. For the sake of public good, folk songs are forbidden henceforward. All and sundry must take heed or ignore this notice at your own peril!

Third Sister (*mirthfully*):

Up in the heavens, lesser lights gravitate towards great ones;

Down on earth, the lion reigns supreme in his kingdom.

Emperors summons all courtiers for a session.

We are fearless freemen while we sing.

(*The crowd joins in the last two lines.*)

Third Sister: Fellow countrymen, let us go and sing.

Lord Mo (*scowling*): Don't you dare!

Crowd: Let's go and start singing.

Third Sister: Come on, let's go and sing.

Lord Mo (*in a panic-stricken gabble*): How... dare... you!

Third Sister (*thematically*):

Life is sad without songs. (*Exit.*)

Crowd (*at the top of their voices*):

We sing to air some protests and vent our share of anger;

A road less travelled is overgrown with rank grass;

Whetstones are useful when your knife goes rusty;

To fix a hunchback, walk always with your head held high.

(*The Steward and the servants chase Third Sister.*)

Lord Mo (*in utter desperation*): Fellow countrymen and neighbors...

Crowd (*in high spirits*):

　　　　山歌好比春江水，

　　　　深山老林处处流，

　　　　若还有人来阻挡，

　　　　冲破长堤泡九州。

莫海仁　州官大人既已下令禁歌，我看还是不唱为妙。

　　　　三姐拿伞从群众中出。

三　姐　（唱，众和）

　　　　好笑多，

　　　　好笑州官禁山歌，

　　　　锣鼓越打声越响，

　　　　山歌越禁歌越多。

　　　　歌声中莫进财上，说："老爷，刘三姐不见了。"莫海仁说："拿
　　　　伞的那个就是。"莫进财又朝拿伞姑娘的方向追去。

三　姐　（唱，众和）

　　　　山顶有花山脚香，

　　　　桥下有水桥面凉，

　　　　心中有了不平事，

　　　　山歌如火出胸膛。

莫海仁　不准唱!

三　姐　（又在群众中唱，众和）

　　　　唱起山歌好种田，

　　　　不费功夫不费钱，

　　　　一不偷来二不抢，

　　　　众人唱歌大过天。

Our songs gush like an everlasting spring,

Such as one can chance upon in the hills and woods.

Anyone tries to halt it, and it explodes,

Flooding all the way, deluging all the land.

Lord Mo (*mortified, with finality*): Since the magistrate has forbidden singing, I

think it would be wise for you to give up.

(*Third Sister emerges from the crowd with an umbrella.*)

Third Sister (*defiantly while the crowd joins in the crowd*):

Hilarity! In superlatives indeed!

Magistrates out against us law-binding villagers!

On a most untenable pretext not known to the annals of history.

Yet the more you forbid us, the more we will sing!

(*The Steward returns during the singing and reports: "Sir, Third Sister has
disappeared." Lord Mo tells him: "The girl with the umbrella. Don't lose track
of her." The steward pursues the girl with the umbrella.*)

Third Sister (*iconoclastically while the crowd joins in the singing*):

Flowers at the hilltop breathe fragrance into space.

Waters flowing brings a cooling effect all around.

Should injustice rankle in the heart,

My songs burst out like fire.

Lord Mo (*snarling*): I forbid you to sing!

Third Sister (*undaunted, comes out singing from the crowd*):

Singing affords a sort of cost-free release from daily strain,

Reflecting our fondest dreams and aspirations,

Sorely needed to survive in such troubled times,

Without stooping to banditry or sinking into depravity.

群众围住"三姐"合唱最后二句，莫海仁从群众中把"三姐"拉出。

莫海仁　刘三姐！

莫进财　（拉一拿伞女群众上）老爷，这哪里是刘三姐！
　　莫海仁一看两个都是服饰与三姐相同的女子，气极，摔开。刘三姐从另一堆群众中唱出。

三　姐　（唱，众和）
　　我唱山歌你抓人，
　　再唱一首给你听。
　　穷人嘴巴封不住，
　　要想禁歌万不能。（下。）

小　牛　（唱，众和）
　　刀砍杉树不死根，
　　火烧芭蕉不死心，
　　刀砍人头滚下地，
　　滚上几滚唱几声。

莫海仁　不准唱！
　　四处歌声起。

众　人　（唱）
　　大雨蒙蒙不见天，
　　大河涨水不见船，
　　四处歌声不见姐，
　　引得狐狸四处钻。
　　莫海仁气得发昏。

(*People surround Third Sister fending her off while repeating the refrains. Lord Mo seizes another girl, mistaking her for Third Sister.*)

Lord Mo (*in a daze*): Ha, Third Sister!

(*Enter the steward bringing a girl with an umbrella.*)

Steward (*yelling hysterically*): Sir, this isn't Third Sister!

(*Lord Mo sees that neither girl is Third Sister, but both are wearing the same dress as hers. He pushes them furiously aside. Third Sister comes out leading another group singing.*)

Third Sister (*protesting while the crowd joins in*):

I keep on singing despite being pursued by your lackeys;

Here's another admonition for you:

You can never seal off our tongues,

If one voice is stilled, there are still plenty more. (*Exit.*)

Xiaoniu (*taking the lead while the crowd joins in*):

When you cut the cedar its root survives,

When you burn the banana its heart lives on;

Cut a man's head, and it rolls on the ground,

Even then it will go on singing till the last breath!

Lord Mo (*bursting out again*): I forbid you to sing!

(*Songs pour out from all quarters.*)

Crowd (*triumphantly*):

A downpour will darken the sky,

A rising tide deters all fishing on the river;

A singing Third Sister is everywhere but nowhere to be found——

Even the most treacherous fox has no clue to her whereabouts.

(*Lord Mo is nearly choking with fury.*)

兰芬、冬妹等（唱）

> 气死他，
>
> 气得螃蟹满地爬，
>
> 四面八方歌声响，
>
> 气死财主老王八。

莫海仁　你们这帮小穷鬼也敢唱歌骂我！

三　姐（忽而出现在榕树脚的石头上，唱）

> 小小公鸡尾婆娑，
>
> 穷人代代爱唱歌，
>
> 唱得天旋地也转，
>
> 财主官家莫奈何。

莫海仁　你竟敢目无官府，违抗禁令！

三　姐（唱）

> 富人少来穷人多，
>
> 锁住苍龙怕什么，
>
> 剥掉龙麟当瓦盖，
>
> 砍下龙头垫柱脚，
>
> 力不穷来智不尽，
>
> 敢和龙王动干戈。

> 小牛一箭把禁令射落。

众　人（唱）

> 富人少来穷人多，

Lanfen and Dongmei (*jauntily*):

> Let him fume at what has happened,
>
> In rage the crabs scuttle around;
>
> Let our free-spirited songs ring in all directions,
>
> May the old scoundrel utter sighs of despair!

Lord Mo (*completely deflated*): So you miserable rioters dare to revile me with your songs!

Third Sister (*suddenly appearing on a rock under the banyan tree*):

> The cockerel grows a handsome tail,
>
> The poor will raise and make the most of their voices;
>
> They sing till heaven and earth spin dizzy,
>
> And the wicked and the rich are thrust forth like worthless trash!

Lord Mo (*at his wits' end*): How dare you defy the authority of the Yamen?

Third Sister (*cheerfully and jauntily*):

> Few are the rich, many the poor;
>
> We sing, while the wicked being at their wits end.
>
> Though all the kings on the earth did show,
>
> Their uppermost power and strength,
>
> They could not seal off our lips,
>
> Our greatest sufferings here wo do sing out,
>
> We, who alone at last, and often,
>
> Know that our strength is infinite, our power, boundless——
>
> And we dare to sing, live, dream, prevail!
>
> (*Xiaoniu aims at the magistrate's injunction and shoots it down.*)

Crowd (*chortling*):

> Few are the rich, many the poor;

锁住苍龙怕什么，

剥掉龙头垫住脚，

力不穷来智不尽，

敢和龙王动干戈。

莫海仁 （手执禁令，浑身颤抖）来呀！与我把刘三姐抓起来！

　　　　家丁执匕首上，群众阻挡，三姐从人群中冲出。

三　姐 （唱）

山崩地裂我不怕，

水泡九州我不惊，

遍地都有歌声响，

哪怕财主谋害人。

莫海仁 来呀！与我拿下！

小　牛 莫海仁，（一箭将莫海仁的帽子射落）你小心了！

　　　　群众欢呼。莫海仁失魂落魄，狼狈不堪，与众家丁下。

　　　　——中幕落

众　人 （在中幕前唱）

唱山歌，

一人唱来万人和，

唱得穷人哈哈笑，

唱得财主打哆嗦。

We sing, while the wicked being at their wits end.

Though all the kings on the earth did show,

Their uppermost power and strength,

They could not seal off our lips,

Our greatest sufferings here wo do sing out,

We, who alone at last, and often,

Know that our strength is infinite, our power, boundless——

And we dare to sing, live, dream, prevail!

(*Shaken, Lord Mo picks up the order.*)

Lord Mo (*considerably devastated*): Here, men! Arrest Third Sister.

(*Enter servants armed with daggers. The crowd will not let them approach Third Sister, who escapes under the cover of the crowd.*)

Third Sister (*distinctly*):

I will not tremble even if the sky falls;

Neither will I shudder at the approach of a deluge.

Third Sister has never been afraid of death;

A murderous local tyrant like Mo does not silence me!

Lord Mo (*snarling himself hoarse*): Here! Arrest her!

Xiaoniu: Look out, Mo Hairen! (*He shoots off Lord Mo's hat.*)

(*The crowd cheers. The terrified Lord Mo withdraws with hisunderlings.*)

(*The inner curtain goes down.*)

Crowd (*carnivalesquely before the inner curtain*):

Let us sing loud and out strong;

With open mouths our strong melodious songs.

We sing till the poor rejoice,

Till the wicked tremble with fear.

老渔翁 老二，我看莫海仁这老狗不会善罢甘休！

刘　二 是呀！恐怕官家还会派兵前来……

外乡人 三姐，请你马上离开这里，到我们那里去。

兰　芬 到你们那里做什么？

外乡人 到我们那里去传歌！

　　　　众外乡人齐要求三姐去传歌。

刘　二 三妹，你和小牛走吧！你们要到处走，到处唱，把穷人的心都
　　　　唱开！

三姐、小牛　二哥，你呢？

刘　二 你们放心地走吧！这里天大的事有我。

群　众 对！有我们大家。

兰　芬 三姐，你教我们的歌，我们要永远唱下去。

众　人 （唱）
　　　　唱尽人间不平事，
　　　　唱出穷人一片心，
　　　　唱得一禾生九穗，
　　　　唱得黑夜太阳红。

Old Fisherman: Liu'er, I don't think Mo Hairen will leave it at that.

Liu'er (*taking in the situation, almost simultaneously*)**:** I agree. I'm afraid the corrupt magistrate, in league with Mo, may send his soldiers...

Stranger: Third Sister, we urge you to leave here at once. Come to our place.

Lanfen (*chiming in*)**:** Why to your place?

Stranger: We will afford them refuge. In the slack season they will teach us songs.

> (*All the strangers implore Third Sister to go with them and promise to take them in in exchange for her musical coaching.*)

Liu'er: We will here part company, sister and Xiaoniu. Find a safe haven first. Truth is not honored in these days. Wherever you happen to be, sing and hearten all the poor brethren.

Third Sister and Xiaoniu: What's your plan for life, brother?

Liu'er: Don't worry. I will move on. Just pray less tribulations and dangers lie ahead of you in life.

Crowd: Hurrah! You can depend on us in case!

Lanfen: Sister, we shall always sing the songs you've taught us.

Crowd (*carnivalesquely*)**:**

> Of our hearts we will sing, oft and long,
>
> Nobody will still our brave music, come what may;
>
> We shall sing until justice rolls down like waters,
>
> And happiness like a mighty stream.

尾声　传歌

众　人（唱）

　　　　送姐送到大江河，

　　　　乘风破浪去传歌，

　　　　财主听见心头跳，

　　　　穷人听见笑哈哈。

　　　　在歌声中三姐、小牛上了老渔翁的小船。

三　姐（唱）

　　　　乘风破浪去传歌，

　　　　刀山火海当平坡，

　　　　天下穷人心一条，

　　　　一人唱歌万人和。

众　人（唱）

　　　　一人唱歌万人和，

　　　　唱得江水滚金波，

　　　　江水滚滚流不尽，

　　　　千年万代不断歌。

　　　　——幕落·全剧终

ACT EIGHT   EPILOGUE
Third Sister on Her Thorny Road to Glory

Crowd (*tenderly and proudly, reluctant to part*):

Third Sister's roaming among many lands is popular lore,

Our regal songbird knows all about singing and more,

After numerous tribulations and danger in life,

Bells will ring out at her triumphant return to her native soil.

(*Amid the singing, Third Sister and Xiaoniu board the old fisherman's little boat.*)

Third Sister (*exulting in a sense of pride in empowering and ennobling her own people*):

Third Sister is bound on her thorny road to glory,

My music with a message proves the folks' joy.

And my spirit flies on powerful wings,

Lifting my nations's reputation to the moon and stars.

Crowd (*gratefully and triumphantly*):

Third Sister is deeply revered in this sphere,

Singing is the tangible expression of our free soul.

The green hills stay and rivers roll on——

Where her undying songs forever echo.

(*Curtain. The end.*)

第二部分　彩调剧中的刘三姐歌谣

Part Two　Liu Sanjie Mountain Songs in Liuzhou Caidiao Opera

第二部分歌谣唱段选自彩调剧《刘三姐》(第三方案，1959年7月)、彩调剧《刘三姐》(第八稿，1978年1月)。两个剧本均根据邓昌伶同名剧本改编，编剧为曾昭文、龚邦榕、邓凡平、牛秀、黄勇刹、包玉堂。

All the lyrics and verses in this part are culled from the third edition of Caidiao Opera Liu Sanjie, printed in July, 1959, the eighth edition of Caidiao Opera Liu Sanjie, revised in January, 1978. Both editions were collectively written by Zeng Zhaowen, Gong Bangrong, Deng Fanping, Niu Xiu, Huang Yongcha and Bao Yutang, inspired by the namesake script created by Deng Changling.

1

序歌：

柳州有个鱼峰山，

山下有个小龙潭，

终年四季歌不断，

歌仙美名天下传。

Prelude：

In the vicinity of the Liuzhou city, there are two famed retreats,

Fish Peak Hill and Little Dragon Pond which draw droves of visitors.

Each year to pay homage to a Goddess of Singing,

Held in the highest esteem and deepest veneration.

2

刘三姐：

柳江河水浪滔滔，

三姐坐藤水上漂，

急水滩头唱一句，

风平浪静姐逍遥。

Third Sister：

Waves tumble and swirl,

Third Sister drifts along on a makeshift raft of vines,

On occasion I sing out to steer clear of some rapids,

To calm down while savoring the scenic beauty on both banks.

3

老渔翁：

金鸡听见金鸡叫，

凤凰听见凤凰啼，

哪个歌声这样美，

唱哑我这老画眉。

Old Fisherman：

Golden cock crow far and wide,

Phoenixes are calling out presaging the arrival of a rare guest from afar.

A veteran singer, I am totally bewitched,

By what I have heard on the river.

4

刘三姐：

风平浪静姐逍遥，

河里鱼虾都来朝，

树上鸟儿都来拜，

都来要姐把歌教。

Third Sister：

Barely recovered from my fright, I find waters less turbulent,

Whence fish and prawn swarm up to pay their respects,

Birds flock circling overhead saluting me with eyes,

So that they could take some music lessons with me.

刘三姐：

财主越怕我越唱，

口口声声唱不停，

唱尽人间不平事，

唱到黑夜太阳明。

Third Sister：

The more the wicked become apprehensive of my songs,

The more I will keep singing them out.

I can't bear to see so much grief and human suffering around;

Such is my tender but modest complaint.

刘三姐：

有缘有缘真有缘，

漂江遇着打鱼船；

老渔翁：

接得三姐我家住，

龙潭村边把歌传。

Third Sister：

Karma turns up that I have at last encountered a fishing boat,

Whereupon there must be strangers willing to bail me out.

Old Fisherman：

I am only too willing to entertain an angel,

Accommodating her so that she will teach us some songs.

7

兰芬：

小龙潭水清悠悠，

成群鱼儿水中游，

妹摆衣裳鱼摆尾，

妹唱山歌鱼抬头。

Lanfen：

Crystal clear is the Little Dragon Pool,

Wherein fish swarm and swim leisurely,

Keeping company while I am washing clothes,

Fish thrilling and nodding in glee.

8

李小牛：

今天打鱼闯着鬼，

打得一只癞头龟，

送给财主当鱼税，

养在灶脚好扒灰。

Li Xiaoniu：

No sooner have I cast my net than I have drawn in a turtle!

Bad omen indeed! There is a better purpose served, a good idea entertained,

That I will give it out to the local tyrant,

So that he would be a cuckold.

9

李小牛:

屙屎下塘气死狗,

青草烧灰气死牛,

河里打鱼潭里放,

气得老猫眼泪流。

Li Xiaoniu:

Dogs fume as the pond becomes somebody's urinal;

Cattle herd have been enraged because his favorite grass is burned into ashes;

Fish caught with so much ado is set alive.

Such senseless acts even make old cats exasperate.

10

李小牛:

打铁不怕火星飙,

唱歌不怕杀人刀,

三姐唱倒阎王殿,

我敢唱断奈何桥。

Li Xiaoniu:

Blacksmith strikes iron despite sparks flying in the air;

Singers are not deterred by a ban lifted on music.

Sanjie's singing echoes across the upper and lower regions,

While all the persecutors and villains are destined for oblivion.

11

刘三姐：

柳江河水弯又长，

不是莫家养鱼塘，

河里鱼虾众人有，

强收鱼税太荒唐。

Third Sister：

Long and bountiful flows the Liujiang River;

Heaven frowns upon any attempt to seize it for private end.

Fish and prawn are common prey up for the catching;

A tax levied upon harvesting is out of the question.

12

刘三姐：

大路不平旁人踩，

情理不合众人抬，

扁担不直用刀砍，

眼见不平口就开。

Third Sister：

When a road is rough, we tread it.

We reason with somebody who defies reasoning.

A crooked carrying pole must be pared to size.

Popular grievances make perfect themes for singing.

13

刘三姐：

上山有棍打得蛇，

下河有网捉得鳖；

有理敢把皇帝骂，

管你老爷不老爷！

Third Sister：

Slay a serpent with a staff,

Catch a turtle when you have a net to cast.

Curse the Emperor as he misrules the country.

Justice we trust and fight for, come what may.

14

刘三姐：

覃家财主要我死，

河里鱼虾要我活，

河里鱼虾把我救，

要我四海去传歌。

Third Sister：

The vicious lord means me the ultimate harm,

While fish and prawns come to my rescue.

I owe my life to these good-hearted creatures,

So that I can spread songs to the end of the world.

15

老渔翁：

不怕风卷千层浪，

我敢撑船漂大洋，

千层恶浪我不怕，

留下三姐又何妨！

Old Fisherman：

Stormy rivers and mighty torrents occur in my career,

An experienced boatman readily sets out ocean-going.

Surviving so many shipwrecks, braving so many rough currents,

I will harbor this special fugitive with utmost honor.

16

李小牛：

龙潭村边树木多，

树高引得凤凰落，

留得三姐村中住，

鱼也多来歌也多。

Li Xiaoniu：

Dragon Pool Village abounds in woods.

Tall trees exert a pull on phoenixes to alight.

Sanjie should be well accommodated with care utmost,

So that the well-being of all the villagers be ensured.

17

众：

年年中秋是歌节，

木叶歌声满山间，

木叶吹得山也笑，

歌声唱得月更圆。

Crowd：

Each year, Singing Festival falls on Mid-Autumn,

Filling every nook and cranny of the village with sweet melodies,

Amid reed flute being played to the merriment of hills,

And the full moon beams up in the starry sky.

18

兰芬：

相思树上画眉叫，

等哥不到妹心焦，

眼中流出相思泪，

汗巾抹烂好几条。

Lanfen：

A wood thrush is warbling from the branch.

You have kept me waiting for so long, my lad,

In tears and ever-heightened anxiety,

That I have run out of handkerchiefs for a better view.

19

亚木：

石崖顶上兰花开，

半夜想妹半夜来，

老虎走先我走后，

脚踩南蛇当草鞋。

Yamu：

Orchid blooms at the peak top.

I will meet my girl even in the dead of night,

At a rendezvous haunted by tigers and snakes,

With hardly any human trace, super good for lovers hating being spied on.

20

李小牛：

引妹唱，

清潭起浪引鱼来，

花开引得蝴蝶到，

哪个敢上唱歌台？

Li Xiaoniu：

I will take the lead.

Fish swarm into a rippling pond;

Butterflies flock to the flowers in blossom.

Let me introduce Sanjie to the audience.

21

冬妹：

水泻滩头哗哗响，

妹不见哥心就忧；

喝茶连杯吞下肚，

千年不烂记心头。

Dongmei：

Waters roar off a rapid,

Startling the maid lovesick for her boy;

With her fancy so out of bounds,

She even gulps down tea to the dregs.

22

兰芬：

天天走过藕塘边，

眼望莲藕心想莲（连）；

铜打肝肠都想断，

铁打眼睛也望穿。

Lanfen：

I walk by the lotus root ponds each day,

Eye upon the water plant but totally absent minded.

A Lovesick lad pines for his lass,

Heart of iron and eye of steel wearing out.

23

亚木等:

金丝绣球鲜又鲜,

千针万线妹手连,

哥接绣球胸前挂,

条条线把哥心牵。

Yamu with others:

Embroidered balls are the keepsake of love,

Embroidered to knit and tie two hearts proved.

I nab and bear the ball and walk out,

Solid proof of fidelity that lasts.

24

众:

什么吃草不吃根?

什么吃草连连吞?

什么肚里有牙齿?

什么肚里走马灯?

Crowd:

What eats grass but forgoes its root?

What gulps down both grass and root ?

What has a belly with teeth?

What has a running horse lantern within?

25

兰芬：

镰刀吃草不吃根，

锄头吃草连根吞，

磨子肚里有牙齿，

风车肚里走马灯。

Lanfen：

Sickles eat grass but dispense with roots.

Hoes indiscriminately consume both grass and root.

Millstones are equipped with internal teeth.

A winnow, a running horse lantern within.

26

刘三姐：

莫夸多，

凤凰莫夸小阳雀，

土岭怎与高山比，

小溪怎能比大河？

Third Sister：

You are flattering me!

Phoenixes are taunting a small finch.

A small ridge is dwarfed by a lofty mountain.

A small brook is no match for a mighty river.

27

老渔翁：

不是出门不唱歌，

是怕三姐山歌多，

只因三姐唱得好，

山头鸟儿不敢歌。

Old Fisherman：

Modesty compels me to sing no more,

Since we boast of an unusual talent in the neighborhood,

Whose musicianship surpasses all the local singers combined.

Reckoning this uncanny human, birds think twice before tweeting.

28

刘三姐：

满天乌云你讲亮，

檀香你讲是木糠，

李小牛：

蚂拐（青蛙）躲在尿桶底，

人家讲臭你讲香。

Third Sister：

What a contrarian you are!

It's sunny outside, but you see dark clouds billow in the sky;

You mistake a piece of sandalwood for sawdust;

Li Xiaoniu：

And your nose fools you into praising,

Armies of pests crawling by a urinal which stinks.

29

众：

铁算盘，

一斗借来五斗还，

莫家算盘一声响，

穷人眼泪流不完！

Crowd：

A shrewd abacus, heartless indeed!

Woe to any debtor of this loan shark!

The moment beads of the usurer's abacus are stirred up,

Tears stream down the cheeks of the poor on end.

30

刘三姐：

我唱山歌大家和，

如今世道荒唐多，

有钱人家高楼大厦无人住，

穷苦人家无房无舍住庙角。

Third Sister：

My songs prove an outburst of popular discontent,

Attesting to the elemental fact of disparities wherein poor folk bears the brunt.

Rich people own so many properties left vacant,

While the most miserable among us sleep outside the temple.

31

刘三姐：

我唱山歌大家和，

如今世道荒唐多，

有钱人家骑马坐轿喊腰痛，

穷苦人家肩膀磨烂苦难说。

Third Sister：

I sing to remonstrate against the excesses borne by the poor,

Destined to lose out in such a hideous status quo,

Wherein the rich in a sedan chair complain of an arduous walking,

And his poor cousins skewer at such oft-absurd human condition.

32

刘三姐：

我唱山歌大家和，

如今世道荒唐多，

有钱人家五黄六月穿绸缎，

穷苦人家十冬腊月打赤膊。

Third Sister：

I sing in protestation of the seamy side of life,

Wherein our complaint must be heard despite the zany magistracy.

The rich clad in silk through four seasons are a selfish breed,

As they shut their eyes to the sad sight of many in rags in bitter winter.

33

刘三姐：

我唱山歌大家和，

如今世道荒唐多，

有钱人家逢年过节杀猪宰羊祭天地，

穷苦人家年三十晚逃租躲债泪成河。

Third Sister：

Finally, I sing and grumble on your behalf,

The rich wallow in gross pleasantries and feasts to our mortification.

Enough is enough, the vanities of the rich, the miseries of the poor,

Whose memories are still filled with former times' rebellious lore.

34

兰芬、李小牛：

讲起黄连嘴就苦，

讲起杨梅心就酸。

讲起财主莫怀仁，

怒火烧身咬牙关!

几时等到东风起?

吹开乌云见青天!

Lanfen and Li Xiaoniu:

Bitter-wort is bitter in name and in deed;

My heart saddens with the mention of a sea of troubles we have to endure.

The foremost butt of our hatred is Lord Mo;

All the mischief he does disqualifies him to the epithet of humanity.

Everybody expects the east wind to rise,

Dispelling the clouds, giving way to clear, broad daylight.

35

刘三姐:

蓬柴起火高万丈,

大海翻风浪滔天;

人多推山山也倒,

人多戽海海也干。

只要穷人心连紧,

总有一天见青天。

Third Sister:

Fagots burn, with flames soaring into the sky.

A stormy sea tosses up billows upon billows.

We are many and they are few.

In case we must drain the sea, we are sure it will go dry.

Nobody will hush our cries of pain and grief,

We must all stand up to seek redress and relief.

36

莫怀仁：

良田万顷我嫌少，

老婆九个不嫌多，

谷仓胀破我不怕，

最怕穷人唱山歌。

Lord Mo Huairen：

With ten thousands of hectares of good farmland in my possession,

An enviable entourage of nine wives at my bidding,

Plus a barn bulging with rice, all to satisfy my vanity.

There is only one thing I detest: songs sung out to incite popular groaning.

37

幕后歌声：

金丝绣球镶红豆，

暗地相思哥不知。

雨里蜘蛛来结网，

想晴（情）唯有暗中丝（思）。

Choir Backstage：

Edge and trim the embroidered ball with red beans,

Token of my love for the lad still in the dark.

Spiders spin their webs in the rain,

Alas! I pine for sowing my love in secret.

38

刘三姐：

姐纺棉，

耕种纺织不得闲，

自己纺来自己染，

自己缝来自己穿。

边纺棉纱边唱歌，

一条银线飞过河。

分明妹子在讲话，

又怪妹子在唱歌。

Third Sister：

I am at weaving a piece of cloth,

Barely out of the fields for some house chores.

I will both weave and dye and cut,

A dyer, weaver and dressmaker all in one!

Humming out a tune, I keep spinning a yarn,

Some threads invisible, but connected to someone I adore.

Am I thinking to myself？

Or am I singing out of tune？

刘二：

唱首山歌解心忧，

喝口凉水浇心头，

凉水解得心头火，

唱歌解得万般愁。

Liu'er：

I sing a song to appease my love-sickness,

And drink cold water to cool my hot head.

Cold water helps me turn around this tricky phase;

Songs dissolve sorrows in no small measure.

刘三姐：

几多家财我不爱，

哪个瞎眼乱跑来，

一张破席将他卷，

三块土皮倒顶埋。

Third Sister：

Wealth entices me not so much,

As my love for the boy I adore.

Confounded be the matchmaker making a mess of my situation,

As I value true affection above anything else.

刘三姐：

可恨财主诡计多，

说亲不成把人捉，

当众破开墨鱼肚，

一眼看穿黑心窝。

Third Sister：

The devilish lord, with so many ruses and guile up his sleeves,

Has nabbed me into custody due to my turning down his marriage offer.

Gut him, and you will see:

He has a heart as black as that of a cuttlefish.

刘三姐：

好心多，

狐狸跑来修鸡窝，

葫芦装的什么药？

分明怕我唱山歌！

Third Sister：

No more of your cajolery!

A fox turns a sponsor of chicken coops.

What axe on earth you have to grind?

I surmise what you fear and abhor the most is my songs!

43

众：

凤是凤来鸡是鸡，

不会唱歌你莫啼，

泥鳅跌进石灰罐，

不死也要脱层皮！

Crowd：

A cock is a cock, not to be confused with a phoenix.

We don't reckon a cock's crowing as proper act of singing.

Too late even you want to give up,

A loach landed into a lime pit,

you are dead or mortally ill even though you manage to escape.

44

刘三姐：

一把芝麻撒上天，

肚里山歌万万千，

唱到京城打个转，

回来还唱十把年。

Third Sister：

One handful of sesame seeds tossed into the air,

I have songs immediate for retrieval or improvisation.

I could sing all the way to the imperial capital back and forth,

Then for another ten years or more.

45

刘三姐：

未曾吃酒先摆杯，

未曾下雨先打雷，

对歌先通名和姓，

无名无姓懒得回。

Third Sister：

Set the table before a feast is ready.

Thunder precedes shower as a rule.

For courtesy's sake,

Please let us have your names.

46

刘三姐：

姓陶不见桃结果，

姓李不见李花开，

姓罗不见锣鼓响，

三个蠢材哪里来？

Third Sister：

I don't see peach trees bear any fruit.

Nor do I see plum blossom in my front.

The mute guy by the name of Gongs, sound!

For even a dumbard dares challenge me!

47

李秀才：

你莫狂，

孔子面前卖文章，

麻雀也与凤凰比，

种田哪比读书郎。

Scholar Li：

Barbarity!

Peddling your learning before our patron saint Confucius?

A sparrow cannot compare with the royalty of phoenix,

Neither can a farmhand, with a scholar well versed in the Confucian canon!

48

三姐：

你逞强，

你想骑马上屋梁，

问你几时下谷种？

问你几时谷子黄？

Third Sister：

Flaunting your seeming superiority!

Riding a horse all the way up the roof？

Here's the ABC for a would-be scholar:

When are the proper times for reaping and sowing?

49

陶秀才：

硬逞强，

耕种本是小名堂，

九月重阳下谷种，

十二月天谷子黄。

Scholar Tao：

Bullshit!

Farming is well beneath our lofty scholastic pursuits.

In September we sow the seeds.

Harvest comes in December.

50

外地歌手：

什么生来头戴冠，

大红锦袍身上穿？

什么生来肚子大，

手脚不分背朝天？

Singers from a Neighboring Village：

Who is born with a hat on, robed in red with brocade embroidery?

Who is born with a potbelly, legs and feet folded together,

Crawling on all fours, with back hunched against the sky?

51

三秀才：

中了状元头戴冠，

大红锦袍身上穿，

老爷享福肚子大，

拜见官府背朝天。

Three Scholars：

When a would-be scholar passes the imperial examination,

He is entitled to court protocols regarding apparel and decorations.

And when a pleasure-filled overlord pays homage to a powerful magistrate,

He grovels on his belly and hails his superiors.

52

刘三姐：

你发癫，

我问地来你答天，

为何天上有风雨？

为何地上有山川？

Third Sister：

You have gone insane,

Having strayed from our topic agreed. Talk of heaven as you ought to.

Who conjures up wind and rain in the sky?

Who sees to it there are hills and streams on earth?

兰芬：

柳江是条清水河，

你的歌书臭气多，

莫把歌书丢下去，

免得弄脏这条河。

Lanfen：

Note this is a clear river by which we stand.

It behooves we all restrain from littering or fouling it.

The least with your songbooks that stink so much——

A veritable hazard to the clean waters.

刘三姐：

唱我不过快回去，

回去再学十把年，

学了十年再来唱，

免得出丑太可怜！

Third Sister：

Since I have carried the day and outsung you three,

It seems you are left with only one option:

Turn tail, flee home, practice one more decade,

Before you are urged or hired to challenge me again.

55

众：

笑你癫来笑你疯，

灯草架桥枉费工，

乌鸦想与凤同林，

竹篮打水一场空。

Crowd：

That must be the tall tale for years to come,

When three stuffy scholars attempt to build a bridge with hay.

A magpie passes off for a phoenix, all the efforts proved futile,

As drawing in water with a leaking basket.

56

众：

好笑多，

好笑老牛跌下河，

若还老牛泡死了，

拿起刀仔慢慢剥。

Crowd：

Hilarity! To the highest degree!

A doddering old bovine stumbles into the river!

Should he really be drown,

We'll have his hide flayed bit by bit!

众：

蛇毒就算竹叶青，

人毒不过莫怀仁，

毒蛇不打伤人命，

坏人不除不太平。

Crowd：

No viper is more venomous then a variety of green bamboo snakes.

No human more inhuman than the local tyrant Mo.

You remain aloof and the snake will stalk you.

You take no arms against evil and it will overtake you.

刘三姐：

梭引线来线跟梭，

手补渔网口唱歌，

手补渔网把歌唱，

鱼满舱来歌满坡。

烂了烂了又来补，

断了断了又来连，

断的连来烂的补，

连连补补用三年。

Third Sister：

We are repairing the used net together,

While leisurely humming a melody.

One stitch in time saves nine,

To ensure a good catch in the days to come.

Fishing nets are meant to be used and repaired.

It is the way things are regarding the business of fishing.

Constant repair and careful usage guarantees,

The usual lifespan of a normal net.

59

刘三姐：

三姐砍柴上山坡，

树木招手鸟唱歌，

河里鱼儿跳出水，

要和三姐对山歌。

Third Sister：

Raising my voice while cutting wood on the hill,

Trees wave their boughs and birds chirp merrily,

Fish leap out of the water,

All itching to have a go with me.

60

刘三姐：

莫唱先，

三姐今天不得闲，

等到中秋歌节夜，

再来和你唱三天。

Third Sister：

Not yet, at least not for today.

Let's set a date till next mid-summer night,

When we will go for a singing spree three days and three nights.

61

李小牛：

三月秧苗岭顶栽，

栽下秧苗望雨来；

新收油麻门前晒，

日晒油麻望口开。

Li Xiaoniu：

March is the season of transplanting rice shoots onto terraced paddies.

That being done, let's cross our fingers for rain.

Newly harvested linseed, sunning out in front of the houses,

Await to crack up before long.

62

李小牛：

韭菜开花一条心，

相见爱姐到如今，

早想同姐传心事，

脚粗手笨不敢亲。

Li Xiaoniu：

As chives' flowers are born straight out from their stems,

So my love for you has always remained constant ever since first sight.

Long have I longed to confess my innermost affection for you, my love,

But for my confounded clumsiness, which always catches me out!

63

刘三姐：

竹子当收你不收，

笋子当留你不留，

绣球当捡你不捡，

捡得忧来捡得愁！

Third Sister：

Harvest bamboo shoots at the right season.

Take this silk ball, token of my love.

Promise me today a union of two hearts.

Or you will regret your prime lost forever.

64

刘三姐：

死乌鸦，

为何窗外叫喳喳，

一箭把你射落地，

丢下大河喂王八。

Third Sister：

Shut up, you damn crow!

Why keep on croaking thus by my window?

Croak on and I'll shoot you down,

And dump you into the river to feed turtles!

65

李小牛：

三两好铁打把刀，

挂在身上动摇摇，

谁人敢把山歌禁，

不断头来也断腰！

Li Xiaoniu：

With the best iron I have three knives hammered out,

Hung by my waist, they embolden me like a warrior.

Anybody sets out to ban Sanjie's singing,

Let him have a test of how sharp my weapon is.

66

刘三姐：

硬要唱，

狐假虎威莫逞强，

若要我们不开口，

除非西边出太阳。

Third Sister：

We choose to ignore your ban.

Stop bullying us. We will never surrender!

We'll never give up singing,

Unless the sun rises in the west and sets in the east.

67

刘三姐：

问一声，

唱歌不挖他祖坟，

行得正来坐得正，

不准唱歌为哪门？

Third Sister：

So, may I ask you——

Did my songs collapse your ancestral graves?

We are decent people, above any mischief,

Ban our songs, and you'll be multiplying your misdeeds.

68

李小牛：

你讲唱歌伤风化，

问你风化是什么？

有伤风化是哪个？

龙潭村头财主家。

Li Xiaoniu：

So you forbid us for the sake of sound morality among lower orders?!

How sound? Are there orders lower than us?

And the sound morality is referred to the village boss's version?

69

刘三姐：

唱歌本是好事情，

不是毒药不害人，

不曾用过水银秤，

为何要怕官大人？

Third Sister：

Singing is truly our entertainment and enlightenment;

As long as we need recreation in improving our miserable lot.

We sing merely to bear up life's indignities with dignity.

Leave us alone, leave us merry making.

70

刘三姐：

又做法师又做鬼，

口吃人肉念弥陀，

勾结官府把歌禁，

借刀杀人更可恶。

Third Sister:

Posing a charitable lord and feinting a promoter of public well-being,

Preying on men while chanting a prayer.

Mo is the meanest character alive we have ever met alive,

That he even sets the magistrate's soldiers against us!

71

李小牛:

刀砍杉树不死根,

火烧芭蕉不死心,

刀砍人头滚下地,

滚上几滚唱几声!

Li Xiaoniu:

You may fell a fir tree, but its roots stay;

You may burn down a plantain's trunk, but its pith remains.

Chop off my head, dare you may;

My songs will go on as I may.

72

刘三姐:

唱起山歌好种田,

不费功夫不费钱,

一不偷盗二不抢,

众：

老子唱歌大过天！

Third Sister：

Singing affords a sort of cost-free release from daily strain,

Reflecting our fondest dreams and aspirations,

Sorely needed to survive in such troubled times,

Crowd：

Without stooping to banditry or sinking into depravity.

73

刘三姐：

我唱山歌你抓人，

再唱一首给你听，

穷人嘴巴封不住，

众：

要禁山歌万不能！

Third Sister：

I am not provoking you. I am only singing.

I will treat my fellow villagers to one more song.

You intend to seal off our mouths.

Crowd：

But I am afraid such roguery will end up in utter futility.

刘三姐：

天崩地裂我不怕，

水泡九州我不惊，

三姐唱歌不怕死，

哪怕狗官百万兵。

Third Sister：

I will not tremble even if the sky falls;

Neither will I shudder at the approach of a deluge.

A born singer, with a divine mission, undaunted by legions of killers,

I will travel to the end of the world singing like never before.

刘三姐：

大河量你舀不尽，

穷人量你杀不完。

柳江水断歌不断，

龙潭水干歌不干。

三姐纵死歌还在，

千年万代唱不完。

Third Sister：

I bet that you cannot scoop a big river out,

Nor decimate the poor from the face of the earth.

Even if the Liujiang River empties, my songs will not;

Even if the Dragon Pool dries up, my voice will go on.

I sense the fate which awaits me,

Yet, as their nightingale, people will forever remember me.

76

刘三姐:

各位乡亲莫挂念,

三姐骑鱼上青天。

年年中秋歌节夜,

再回鱼峰唱一遍。

Third Sister:

Farewell, my own folks, farewell;

Your songbird has become an immortal soaring high on a carp.

Mark this moment and set a date for reunion;

Fish Peak and Dragons Pool are for us all to meet for our singing carnival,

From now on, year after year, generation upon generation.

77

众:

鱼峰山上姐成仙,

山歌留下几千年,

如今广西成歌海,

都是三姐亲口传。

Crowd:

It redounds to her worldly fulfilment that our sister becomes a fairy;

The unsurpassable heritage her people hold to dearest,

Of her free-spirited and wholesome songs,

Enshrined in the hearts of posterity utmost.

第三部分 刘三姐歌谣唱曲译配

Part Three   Musical Scores of the Most Popular Tunes and Lyrics

第三部分唱曲选自《刘三姐》彩调剧及歌舞剧，两种剧本均根据邓昌伶同名剧本改编，编剧为曾昭文、龚邦榕、邓凡平、牛秀、黄勇刹、包玉堂。

Lyrics in this part are culled from Liuzhou Ciaodiao Opera and Musical Drama of Liu Sanjie, which were collectively written by Zeng Zhaowen, Gong Bangrong, Deng Fanping, Niu Xiu, Huang Yongcha and Bao Yutang, based on the namesake opera by Deng Changling.

山歌好比春江水
Songs Like River Waters

1=♭B 2/4 3/4

(3 2 | 1 2 | 3 2 1 6 | 5 - | 5 - | 3 3 2 1 | 6 5 6 1 |

2 1 2 | 6 5 | 5· 6 1 | 2 3 5 6 | 5 -)|

3 2 | 1 2 | 5· 3 | 2· 1 6 | 5· 6 1 | 3 2 3 2 1 |

唱　山　歌　哎——　　　　　　　　这　边
Fo-　llow　me　　　　all　the　way,　on　both

6 5 | 6 1 | 2 6 | 7 6 | 5 - | 5 - |
唱　来　那　边　和。
ri-　ver　banks　we　are　sing- ing　along.

3 3 | 3 3 | 3 5 3 2 | 1 2 | 5· 3 | 2· 1 6 | 5· 6 1 |
山歌　好比　春　江　水　哎——
Like　river　wa- ters my　songs　flow,

3 2 3 | 2 1 | 6 5 | 6 1 | 2 6 | 7 6 | 5 6 1 |
不怕　　滩　险　湾　又　多　啰,
cu- tting　across　shoals　and　skir- ting　bends, and

2 1 2 | 6 5 6 | 5 - | 5 0 ‖
湾　又　多。
skir- ting　bends.

藤 缠 树
Banyan Trees

$1={}^{\flat}B \quad \frac{2}{4}$

(6 1 3 | 3 5 6 5 3 | 5 5 6 | 5 —) |

3 2 3 | 2 2 5 | 6 6 1 | 2·3 2 |
山 中 只 有 藤 缠 树,
Ban- yan tress must be entwined,

2 1 2 | 3 5 6 | 2·3 6 7 6 | 5 — |
世 上 哪 有 树 缠 藤;
vines must cling to banyan trees;

5 5 3 2 | 1 2 3 | 5 3 2·7 6 |
青 藤 那 个 若 是 不 缠 树,
no earthly couples remain more loyal,

1 1 6 5 | 3 5 6 | 1 3 5 | 5 — |
枉 过 那 个 一 春 又 一 春。
for the spring is meant for such a nice end.

(1 1 6 1 6 5 | 3 2 3 5 6 5 6 1 | 5 —) ‖

金丝绣球
Golden Silk Ball

1=C 4/4 小快板、轻快地

（女）

```
5 6 ‖: 2 - - - | 2 2 3 2· 1 | 2 1 6 1 | 6 - |
```
唔　哎——　　　　金　丝　绣　球　鲜　又　鲜，
Wu hei——　　　So bright this embroi- dered ball,

（男）

```
5 6 ‖: 2 - - - | 6 6 1 5· 6 | 5 3 2 3 | 2 - |
```
唔　哎——　　　　金　丝　绣　球　鲜　又　鲜，
Wu hei——　　　This silk ball, a token of my love,

```
2 6 2 1 6 5 | 2 1 6 5 6 - |
```
千　针　万　线　妹　手　连，
count- less stitches I've sewed with my hand,

```
6 5 6 5 3 2 | 2 3 5 6 - |
```
千　针　万　线　妹　手　连，
sewed with golden threads drawn from my heart,

```
2· 5 5 6 6 5 5 0 | 2· 2 6 2 1 6 5 0 |
```
绣　球　飞　过　相　思　树，妹　心　落　在　哥　身　边，
I toss it over the tree of love, catch it lest if fall to the ground,

```
2· 5 5 6 6 5 5 0 | 2· 5 6 6 1 6 5 0 |
```
哥　接　绣　球　胸　前　挂，条　条　线　把　哥　心　牵，
how could I fail to make it, it bangs right at my breast,

妹　心　落　　在　　哥　身　边　啰
my　love,　never　let　it　fall　to　the　ground

条　条　线　把　　哥　心　牵　啰
my　love,　it　bangs　at　my　breast　it　tugs　right-at　my　heart

咧。
le.

咧。
le.

唔
Wu

咧　　唔　哎——
le　　wu　hei——

盘歌——了了啰
A Riddle Verse

1=♭B 2/4 4/4

5· 3 ‖(3 23 22 | 2 16 165 | 0 3 561 |

232 1 656 | 5 — | 5 —)‖ 2 — — — |

（众人）哎——
Ae——
（三姐）哎——
Ae——

3 2	3 2	6 1	2 32	2·	5 3 1	2
什么	水面	打筋	斗 咧？		嘿 了 了	啰！
What fowls	spar u-	pon the	lake?		Hei hei yo	hei!
鸭子	水面	打筋	斗 咧。		嘿 了 了	啰！
Ducks	spar u-	pon the	lake.		Hei hei yo	hei!

3 2	3 2	2 16	165	5·	1 6 3	5
什么	水面	起 高	楼 咧？		嘿 了 了	啰！
What	rises high	on the	ri- ver?		Hei hei yo	hei!
大船	水面	起 高	楼 咧。		嘿 了 了	啰！
Boats	tower	on the	ri- ver.		Hei hei yo	hei!

<u>6</u> <u>1̇</u>　　<u>2̇</u> <u>3̇</u>　　<u>2̇</u> <u>1̇</u>　　<u>2̇ 1̇ 6</u> | 6 <u>1̇</u>　　<u>2̇</u> <u>3̇</u>　　<u>2̇ 1̇ 6</u>　　<u>1̇ 2̇ 1̇</u> |

什么　水面　撑阳　伞 咧?　　什么　水面　共 白 头 咧?

What there- upon keeps out the　sun?　　What water birds make a blessed pair?

荷叶　水面　撑阳　伞 咧。　　鸳鸯　水面　共 白 头 咧。

Lotus　leaves　blind　the sun.　　Man- darin ducks make a model couple.

1̇· 　 <u>3</u>　　<u>3̇ 3̇ 3̇</u>　　<u>2̇ 2̇</u> | <u>2̇ 1̇ 6</u>　　<u>1̇ 6 5</u>　　6 <u>1̇</u>　　<u>2̇ 3̇</u> |

　嗨　什么　　水面　撑阳　伞 咧?　什么　水面

What　there- upon　keeps out　the sun?　　What water birds make

嗨　荷叶　　水面　撑阳　伞 咧。　鸳鸯　水面

Lotus　leaves　　blind the　sun.　　Man- darin ducks make

<u>2̇ 1̇</u>　　<u>6 5</u>　　6　　5· ‖

共　白　头　咧?

a　blessed　pair?

共　白　头　咧。

a　model　couple.

采茶曲
Tea Picking Song

1=F $\frac{2}{4}$ 中速

(6̣3 6̣3 | 6̣3 6̣3 | 5365 353 | 5365 353 | 5365 3512 | ⁵⁄₃3 — |

6561̇ 652 | 6561̇ 652 | 1235 2312 | 6̣ — | 61̇65 66 | 1321 66 |

61̇65 66 | 1321 6̣121 | 6̣·1 5̣7 | 6̣ 60) |

‖: 5365 3 | 2 65 3 | 5 25 | 6̣·5 3 | 5 25 |

春　　天　茶　　叶　嫩　又　　鲜，　　嫩　又

Maids　are　ta-　king　in　the　crop　in　early

6̣·5 3 | 535 321 | 3 2̇· | 53 5351 |

鲜，　　姐妹　双　　双　呵　走　哇　走哇走茶

spring,　ten-　ding　these de-　licate　plants

2321 6̣121 | 65 6̣(1 | 2321 6̣125 | 6757 6̇)| 5365 53 |

园　哟依　哟。　　　　　　　满　山

with　utmost　care.　　　They

2 65 53 | 55 12 | 5 65 3 | 55 12 | 5 65 3 |

茶　树　妹手　种，　　妹手　种，

have　a　rea-son　to　reap the harvest　they

```
5  3    6  5 | 3 5 3   2 2 | 1 3   2 3 | 6̇  − |
辛 勤   换 得   茶 满 园 呵  茶 满        园,
deserve,     tea  aroma  per-meating the    plantations,
```

```
▾  ▾   ▾  ▾              mp                    mf
2 3   1 2 | 3 5   3 2 | 1 3   2 3 | 6̇·1̇  5 7 | 6̇  − |
哪 嗬  依 哎  哟       茶 满    园    哟 依   哟。
la hei  yi ai  yo      per- meating  the    plan- ta-   tions.
```

```
( 2 3 1 2  3 5 6 5 | 3 5 3 2  1 3 2 1 | 6̇·1̇  5 7 | 6̇·1̇  5 7 | 6̇  6 0 ) ‖
```

唱歌好
Born to Sing

1=B $\frac{2}{4}$ $\frac{3}{4}$

♩ = 48

‖:(2̲ 6̣ 7̲ 6̣ | 5̲ 6̣ 1̲ 1 | 2̲ 6̣ 7̲ 6̣ | 5̣ −) |

3̲ 2 ³⁄₄ 1̲ 2 | 5̲ 3 ²⁄₄ 2· 1̲ 6̣ | 5·̣ 6̣ 1 | 3̲ 3 2̲ 1 | 6̣ 5̣ 6̣ 1 |

唱　歌　好　哎,　　　唱出穷　人　嘛
So　en-　chanting songs　　prove,　as heart war-　ming
引　妹　唱　哎,　　　清潭起　浪　嘛
I　will　take the lead for　your　show, fish swarm　into

2̲ 6̣ 7̲ 6̣ | 5̣ − | 3 ³⁄₄ 3 3̲ 3 | 3̲ 5̲ 3̲ 2 1̲ 2 | ²⁄₄ 5̲ 3 2· 1̲ 6̣ | 5·̣ 6̣ 1 |

一　片　心,　山歌好似　松　柏树哎,
like sun-　shine, sing out　loud　and strong as　we　may,
引　鱼　来,　花开引得　蝴　蝶到哎,
a rippling pond, butter- flies flock　　to the flowers,

3̲ 3 2̲ 1 | 6̣ 5̣ 6̣ 1 | 2̲ 6̣ 7̲ 6̣ | 5̣ 6̣ 1 | 2̲ 6̣ 7̲ 6̣ | 5̣ − :‖

敢傲风　雪　嘛　万　年　青啰　万　年　青。
pines endure and　　stand firm in　bitter　winters.
哪个敢　上　嘛　唱　歌　台啰　唱　歌　台。
an instant hit　she　will　become, I am sure.

千年万代不断歌
Undying Songs Forever Echo

$1 = {}^{\flat}\text{B}$ $\frac{2}{4}$

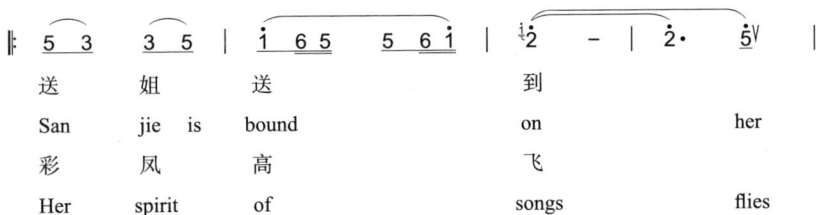

送　姐　送　　　到
San jie is bound　on　her
彩　凤　高　　　飞
Her spirit of　songs　flies

大　江　河　呀，乘　风　破
thor-ny road to glo-ry, her free and whole-some
云　天　外　呀，壮　乡　歌
on power-ful wings, lifting her na-tions

浪　　　去　传　歌。
songs　hear-ten all her people.
海　　　波　连　波。
repu-　tation to the stars.

$\overset{.}{3}$ $\overset{.}{3}\overset{.}{2}$ $\overset{.}{1}$ $\overset{.}{2}$ | $\overset{.}{3}\overset{.}{5}\overset{.}{3}\overset{.}{2}$ $\overset{.}{1}$ $\overset{.}{2}$ | $\overset{.}{5}\overset{.}{3}$ $\overset{.}{2}$ $\overset{.}{1}6$ | $5\cdot6$ $\overset{.}{1}$ |

壮乡　歌 海 波　连　　波，

San jie is deep-ly　re-vered　in this　coun-try,

$\overset{.}{2}$ $\overset{.}{3}$ $\overset{.}{2}\overset{.}{3}\overset{.}{2}\overset{.}{1}$ | $6\overset{.}{1}5$ 6 $\overset{.}{1}$ | $\overset{.}{2}$ 6 7 6 | 5 — |

一 人　　唱　来　万　人　和。

her fame　spreads far　and wide　be-loved　by　all.

$\overset{.}{3}$ $\overset{.}{3}\overset{.}{2}$ $\overset{.}{1}$ $\overset{.}{2}$ | $\overset{.}{3}\overset{.}{5}\overset{.}{3}\overset{.}{2}$ $\overset{.}{1}\overset{.}{2}$ | $\overset{.}{5}\overset{.}{3}$ $\overset{.}{2}$ $\overset{.}{1}6$ | $5\cdot6$ $\overset{.}{1}$ |

江 水　滔滔　流　不　　尽，

The green hills last, ri-　vers　roll　on,

$\overset{.}{3}$ $\overset{.}{2}\overset{.}{3}\overset{.}{2}\overset{.}{1}$ | $6\overset{.}{1}5$ 6 $\overset{.}{1}$ | $\overset{.}{2}\overset{.}{1}\overset{.}{2}$ 656 | 5 — ‖

千 年　万 代　不　断　歌。

wherever her　undying　songs　fore-ver　e-　cho.

后 记

　　作为众多传说、书籍和电影的主题，刘三姐已经成为壮族人民最重要的非物质文化遗产之一、八桂地区的文化符号。相传刘三姐生于唐中宗年间，至今1300多年中，这位高尚的少数民族女杰，利用她的音乐天赋——即兴创作山歌、打抱不平、勇斗智斗贪婪好色的财主，成为中国流行文化中最经久不衰的民间英雄之一。这位歌仙是如何聪慧机敏、歌如泉涌、斗败当地土豪雇用的三位儒家文人的？历史上是否确有刘三姐其人，从而激发了这些经典故事？

　　刘三姐反抗邪恶财主的动力很大程度上源于她个人的遭际和民众对那些欺压佃农的地主的怨恨。她的传奇，也佐证了农耕时代生活不可避免的艰辛残酷的真相。

　　许多人试图证明历史上确有刘三姐其人。根据现有文献资料，关于

Postscript

The subject of legends, books and films, Liu Sanjie has been written indelibly into the cultural heritage of the Zhuang people. Over the course of 1300 years, Liu Sanjie, a high-minded peasant heroine of Zhuang ethnicity——who used her musical talent for improvising mountain songs (shange) to help poor villagers fight against predatory landlords and their lackeys——has become one of the most enduring folk heroes in Chinese popular culture, and one of the most versatile. She is famously said to have outwitted in a contest of song three Confucian literati hired by a local tyrant, but how has the legend of the beautiful and heroic Song Sprite changed shape over time, and did a real Third Sister inspire this and other tales?

In legend and perhaps in life, Liu Sanjie raised her voice against the injustice because of her own hardship; but her songs were also an expression of popular resentment over those oppression of the landed gentry and their maltreatment of their tenants. The legend of Liu exposes the cruelty innate in medieval life.

Numerous attempts have been made to prove that there was a historical

刘三姐最早的文字记载出现在南宋王象之的《舆地纪胜》中，称其刘三妹。从明、清开始，关于刘三姐的描述在文人文本中继续增加。士绅文人通常这样描绘她：自幼擅长笔墨，聪明机智，同时代人莫不称奇，叹为奇人或神童。12岁时，她已精通儒家经典，擅长即兴演唱。当地一位名叫张伟望的学者，慕名约她对歌。这对年轻人棋逢对手，竟夕对歌不舍，七天七夜，遂步入婚姻殿堂，从此幸福地生活在一起（一说共同化为巨石）。

刘三姐在这一类士绅文人叙事中建构的形象，必须在儒家的道德参照系中来理解，因为刘三姐是高雅阶层的一员，而非平民女性，所以刘三姐有权与男性学者交往。这种叙事的政治正确，符合"才子佳人"的儒学传统。

当今流行的版本说刘三姐是一个音乐奇才，出生在广西罗城县的一个小村庄，自小丧父失母，由哥哥抚养长大，兄妹俩相依为生，捕鱼砍柴，家计艰困。刘三姐天生丽质且十分勤奋，她擅长编织，尤擅民歌，少年即以歌闻名。她的歌声，发自肺腑，表达了民怨，歌咏了自由，她勇敢诚实的品质，招致当地土豪莫怀仁的敌意（可以理解，20世纪50年代和60年代制作的关于刘三姐的歌剧和电影都基于这条故事线）。就像卡通里的反派人物一样，莫怀仁竭力想制服这个不羁、自由的女子：他向刘三姐提婚，要把她纳为小老婆（在一夫多妻制的时代，这对一个平民女孩来说是一条有吸引力的社会流动途径），却碰了软钉子。刘三姐提议按壮族习俗，通过对歌决出结果。莫怀仁雇用的三名腐儒，在对歌中嘴笨舌拙，一败涂地。莫怀仁怒不可遏，不惜耗费家财勾结官府，欲把刘三

Liu. The first known literary reference appeared in the Southern Song, referring to her as Liu Sanmei; accounts of her continued to multiply in scholarly texts in the Ming and Qing dynasties. The gentry tradition depicts her as a young woman, skilled in brush and ink, intelligent and quick-witted, hailed by her contemporaries as a prodigy. At twelve she was well versed in the Confucian canons and adept at improvising songs. Out of admiration, a local scholar, called Zhang Weiwang, sought her out for a singing duel. After singing together for seven days, the two married and lived happily ever after. (One version of this story indicates they both turned into boulders.)

The scholar-gentry accounts of Liu Sanjie must to be understood within the moral frame of Confucianism. She is depicted as a member of a well-born class, not a plebian woman, and therefore entitled to associate with male scholars. The political rectitude of this narrative of Liu Sanjie represents her in line with the medieval romantic convention in which a "beautiful lady marries up to gifted scholar".

The popular modern version sees her as a musical wizard, born in a small village in Luocheng county and brought up by her older brother. The siblings scraped together a harsh subsistence, fishing and cutting firewood. Liu was beautiful, diligent, good at weaving, and famous for her angelic voice and musical talent. In this telling of the legend, Third Sister gave voice to popular resentment and communal discontent, incurring the enmity of a local tyrant Mo Huairen (understandably, movies and operas about Liu made in the 1950s and 60s used this version of the story). Like a cartoon villain, Lord Mo tried hard to rein in Liu, making the usual moves of the tyrant upon the maiden: first he made an offer of marriage to take Liu, proposing to take her as one of his concubines (an attractive avenue of social mobility for a commoner girl

姐置于死地而后快。在一个歌圩场合，县衙兵勇前来抓捕刘三姐。刘三姐和她的爱人阿牛，在村民的帮助下得以走脱。然而，为了拯救村民免遭土豪报复，刘三姐甘愿投水自尽。就在她落水的那一刻，一条巨大的金鲤鱼出现了，将她带到了天堂。刘三姐功德圆满，在天上成仙，壮乡人民把她的歌代代相传。

刘三姐在当代是一名高尚的叛逆者，反抗贪婪的地主。她在边缘的民间传说中被发现并转化为壮族人民的代表、最重要的非物质文化遗产之一，这一关键的转换也得到了20世纪50年代政府的大力支持。

1959年，为庆祝中华人民共和国成立十周年，广西壮族自治区政府在南宁组织了一场大规模的文艺会演，着力把刘三姐传奇打造为壮族最重要的非物质文化遗产。据《广西日报》1960年发布的统计数据，来自1209个歌剧团、歌舞团的58000多名演员、歌手接受任务，进行了一次为期20天的会演，当然，绝大多数演职人员都是非专业的，他们以不同剧种表演《刘三姐》，观众超过1200万，占当时广西人口的60%以上。两年后，长春电影制片厂受邀拍摄的同名电影上映，这是中国第一部彩色音乐片，一时风靡全国。

in a time of polygamy for the rich). When Liu rejected him, Mo hired three ineffectual scholars to beat Liu at a singing competition, but she bested them. In fury, Mo enlisted the corrupt local magistrate's soldiers to arrest her during a singing festival. Again, his plan proved abortive: Liu and her lover A Niu fled, helped by villagers. To save the villagers from being attacked on her behalf, Liu jumped into a lake; but the moment she hit the water, a huge golden carp rose and carried Liu to the heavens, where she became an immortal. Villagers then passed down her songs through the generations.

The prevailing treatment of Liu is a high-minded rebel against hawkish lords. In essence, the localized, marginalized, and decentralized folk legend about Liu Sanjie was discovered and transformed into a representation of the Zhuang people, a heroine for a virtuous imagined political community——she is a product, then, of the 1950s' emphasis on folk culture, of the state-sponsored art and literature of that era the early years of the PRC.

To mark the 10th anniversary of PRC, the region's administrators mobilized a massive campaign in Nanning to promote the Liu Sanjie legend as Zhuang's chief intangible asset (intangible cultural heritage, or ICH). According to official statistics released by Guangxi Daily in 1960, in a major effort to foster identity, more than 58000 actors and singers, from 1209 singing and dancing troupes, mostly non-professional, were ordered to put on a 20-day cultural extravaganza across the region——all were cast in the role of "Liu Sanjie" in a variety of dramatic genres. The audience for the event was more than 12 million people, accounting for more than 60 percent of Guangxi's population at that time. The Changchun Film Studio was invited to shoot China's first color musical, a bio-pic on Liu Sanjie two years later. The film was an immediate hit as it squarely established.

将刘三姐打造为广西最重要的非物质文化遗产，经历了一个从民间传说搜集筛选到投演广西彩调剧、歌舞剧，再到电影改编的一系列建构的复杂过程。尽管现代版的刘三姐（毫不奇怪，彩调剧、歌舞剧、电影由区内甚至国内最有才气的文艺工作者创作）取得了非凡的成功，但真实的刘三姐——基于壮族民俗、社会、历史条件的刘三姐传说，更是中国西南山区民众愿望的诗意表达。中国西南地区是典型的民族熔炉，聚集几十个少数民族，这些少数民族，历史上与中央政府时有龃龉，与紧邻的汉族社区关系时有紧张。照例，少数民族通常退往非河谷地区——山上。因此，山歌得名实在有特殊的历史原因。将刘三姐歌咏自由、反抗不公和压迫的主题，置于特定的民俗学环境中，我们将获得更为全面、切题的读解。

　　刘三姐确有其人，但与儒家文人编订或文化建构工程师的建构大异其趣。通过重述、补充和变奏，我们看到了电影中的刘三姐、才子佳人或准革命叛逆者，然而，刘三姐传说核心的核心——一个乡野女性，出生在一个非儒家的环境中，漂亮、机智、能言善辩、憎恨不公正、捍卫自己和族人的自由，仍然是壮族和中国文化传说中最著名的故事之一。

The creation of Liu Sanjie as the region's chief ICH was a complex process, entailing adaptations from folk legends into Guangxi caidiao opera, into music and dance opera, and finally into film. This modern incarnation of Liu, then, must be seen as a phenomenal success. But it built on authentic Liu legends, which had endured for a thousand years. These resilient stories may be seen as the poetic expression of popular aspirations of peoples in the mountainous southwest of China, where a host of ethnic groups are clustered, all of them with a turbulent relationship with mainstream Han populations, and with central imperial governments in ancient times, dedicated to driving the minorities deeper into difficult terrain. It is hard to miss the political themes of freedom and resistance to oppression and exploitation that play in the traditional (and modern) legends of Sanjie, her outsmarting and out-singing of the forces of law and tyrannical order. But a proper account of the Sanjie story should take account of the latest ethno-musical research.

Liu Sanjie did exist, but not in quite the way the Confucian literati or an engineer of nation building would want us to believe. Perhaps it is because of the power and beauty of her songs, and of the culture of the Zhuang, which is enacted in her life and work, that she has been able to be cast, through retellings, adaptations, translations, variations, as so many heroines in many eras across many hundreds of years. Arguable she is all the Liu Sanjies: the glamorous cinematic star, the quasi-revolutionary rebel, the boudoir prodigy, the noble peasant, the feisty beloved—pretty, witty, quick of tongue, independent and proud. The Liu Sanjie we find in her songs is all of these things. Above all, she loathes injustice, she champions freedom for herself and for her community. It is little wonder such a figure, so compellingly human, remains one of the best known tales of both Zhuang and Chinese folklore.

我们可能永远无法断定这位壮族歌仙是否曾在以刘三姐为名的歌曲或传说之外，用血肉之躯呼吸过。即使我们做到了，千千万万的刘三姐粉丝依旧会蜂拥到宜州、柳州或桂林，一探究竟。我们唯一确定的是，这个美丽、自由不羁而聪明的乡野女孩，生活在主流文明外的边缘地带，代表自己的人民歌颂人类自由，与不公正和压迫作斗争，这个题材才是普世性的，具有最深广的吸引力。

作为一位30多年的翻译从业者，笔者对当今学术界不断翻新却无多少实质内容的翻译研究保持戒惧。《圣经》中的"太阳底下无新事"，更多地道出了这个需要匠心的手工活计的本质。17世纪的法国人安娜·达西埃（Anne Dacire）就曾精辟地区别过什么叫"毕恭毕敬的翻译"，什么叫"大开大合的翻译"。她说："第一种翻译，译者毕恭毕敬，刻意追求忠实，实则南辕北辙。此等译者拘守原文造语句序，却无法贯通原文脉络关纽，终至抱形似而失真境，泥皮相而遗神情。如此译来，词既不达，行文阻滞，思致尽失，善读者寓目即辨。大开大合的翻译，忠实原文内容，竭力再现原文的美学特质，并使原文的意象自在自如得以呈现。第二种翻译，全在译者对原著披文入情，会与其心，最后方能手之所至，随意生态（即使大开大合亦不离原文寸步）。如此大笔妙运，一气舒卷，犹如行云流水。不特笔肖原作，而且本身还成了第二原作。这等高手之擅场在此，而且正是其妙造自然庸者所不及处。"本书的翻译，追求行云流水、舒卷自如的境界，希望获得英语读者的认可。

本书的完成有赖于多位朋友、同好鼎力相助，在此一并致谢。

We may never know if Liu Sanjie lived and breathed outside the songs and legends that bear her proud name. Regardless, fans, young and old, flock to Yizhou or Liuzhou or Guilin to tour of her birthplace. What we do know is that the notion of a beautiful and intelligent country woman, who lives on the margins of society, who sings in praise of human freedom, who fights injustice and oppression, has universal appeal—whether she appears on stage in Liuzhou caidiao opera or is played on camera by Huang Wanqiu, or is the young woman to whom so many of the folk songs sung on the shores of Guanxi are attributed: a most charming Goddess of Singing, Liu Sanjie.

A translator for thirty years, fed up with contemporary babble of translations into foreignization versus domestication, literal versus free, etc, I have come to believe the truthfulness of the Biblical adage that there is nothing new under the sun. I fully sign up with a 17th century French translator Anne Dacire when she draws a distinction between "servile translation and a generous translation," the latter she calls "a noble translation that clings closely to the ideas of its original, tries to match the beauty of its language, and renders its images without undue austerity of expression. The first type of translation, the servile one, becomes very unfaithful, because it tries to be scrupulously faithful. It ruins the spirit by trying to save the letter. It is the work of a cold and sterile talent. The second type of translation, on the other hand, which tries above all to save the spirit, does not fail to keep the letter, even where it takes the greatest liberties. With its daring features, which remain always true, it becomes not just the faithful copy of its original, but a second original in its own right. It can only be the work of a writer of genius, solid, noble and productive." I hope the present translation will be deemed a generous one.

Finally, I have to thank a number of people for their help.

当今英语世界最杰出的作家之一马克·特雷迪尼克（Mark Trednnick）先生百忙之中拨冗为歌谣英译润色，并撰写重磅序言，对笔者的译文和对刘三姐的全新解读给予充分肯定，笔者大受鼓舞。笔者长期以来主张汉译英是否合格，必须交由英美高端读者判断，本书的翻译交由英语作家审读润色，就是一个实例。

马克先生著述等身（18种诗歌、散文作品），2008年在当今英语重镇剑桥大学出版过一本关于英语写作的指南（*Writing Well: The Essential Guide*）。马克先生应邀参加过第五期中国国际写作计划，笔者有幸和马克先生朝夕相处一月有余，时时请益，对马克先生大师级的文笔有所领教，钦佩之至。

除此之外，南宁学院张天乾教授、中国海洋大学外国语学院任东升教授参与定稿。后者指派了优秀的研究生焦琳翻译了马克先生惠赐的序言。焦琳同学的译文较好地呈现了当今英语世界自然写作的代表性人物的经典文字。

为了保证译文的可演唱性，笔者最后把乐谱的审稿、定稿工作交由在广西民族大学任教的美国人劳伦斯先生，并和我的上海外院老同学华云一起会商。我们用英文一句一句演唱最脍炙人口的刘三姐歌谣，不断修改，最后请专业人士制作出了乐谱。

重复一句，我的同学华云先生为我的初译提供了关键的英文试唱。

Mark Trednnick, one of the most prominent writers in the English-speaking world, has taken time out of his busy agendas to polish the English translation of the lyrics, and most of all, has written a heavy-weight preface, in which he graciously accords with my translation and my fresh interpretation of Liu Sanjie. My cup of gratitude is full. The author has long dismissed the mainstream translation from Chinese into English being self-churned, self-reviewed and self-consumed, arguing the essence of translation is "to give Chinese authors fair exchange for their characters, not in equal measure but in equal value." I hope I am leading the way in submitting my translation to the reading and polishing of first rate English writers like Mark Trednnick on readability.

Mark is the author of 18 works of poetry and prose, and in 2008 he published Writing Well, a guide to English Writing at Cambridge University. Mr. Mark was invited to participate in the 5th China International Writing Residency. I had the honor to spend more than a month with him, and I stood at his foot marveling how King's English was spoken and written.

In addition, my thanks go to Prof. Zhang Tianqian of Nanning University and Prof. Ren Dongsheng of Ocean University of China for suggesting and supporting the project, and the latter assigned an outstanding graduate student, Jiao Lin, to well translate the masterly preface of Mark Trednnick.

As the project has a two-fold aim, both readable and singable, I must acknowledge my debt to an American professional, L. B. Lawrence, who happens to teach composing in Guangxi University for Nationalities. His comments and suggestions on the musical scores are appropriated in our finalized text.

Above all, thanks to Hua Yun, my classmate in Shanghai Foreign

我们需要的英文歌词必须是开口音、响亮音节，他的试唱就是及时的反馈，能让我当场做必要的修改、换词。这个阶段的工作非常扎实，最后参与乐谱部分审稿、定稿的美国人劳伦斯，对我们前期工作的专业程度大表赞赏。

为了保证英语文字的语法准确，我特邀了在美国哈佛大学教育学院就读的研究生杰瑞·谢（Jerry Xie）对初稿进行了两次审读、校对（发至马克先生润色之前）。谢同学九岁随父母移居加拿大，英语写作，尤其语法修辞细节是其强项。谢同学最初和我合作，约定我译歌谣和歌舞剧剧本，他译电影剧本，我们几乎同时完工，又同时办理授权事宜。我在本城寻到政府相关部门，获得了授权，而谢同学和电影剧本权利人（代理）谈判铩羽而归，使得本书无法收入电影剧本的译文，而这也成了本书最大的遗憾。

最后，衷心感谢国家民委国际交流司原副司长吴金光、省垣音乐界名宿潘荣生、南宁学院副校长陈雄章对本书的持续关注，以及提供的诸多有益建议。

Languages Institute in the late 1970s. To ensure my translated lyrics capable of being sung out, I made him sit by my PC and we moved from sentence to sentence in English, following the musical scores of the most popular lyrics as I made timely alterations and improvements based on his trial singing before we turned to Mr. Lawrence for comments.

To conclude, to make sure the English text is error free (before being sent to Mark Trednnick for reading), I invited Jerry Xie, a post graduate at Graduate School of Education, Harvard University, to proofread the first draft. Xie emigrated to Canada with his parents when he was nine years old. He is good at English writing, almost to the point of being fastidious in grammar and rhetoric. Xie and I initially agreed that I would translate ballads and musicals, and he, the script of movies. We almost finished the work at the same time, and we began to handle the authorization at the same time. In the end, my authorization came off, but his, aborted being declined by the IP owner. That means his love is lost and his beautiful translation fails to be included in this book, the biggest regret of the project.

Mr. Wu Jinguang, former deputy director-general of international exchange department of National Ehnic Affairs Commission, PRC, and Mr. Pang Rongsheng, a veteran musician widely known across the region, and Mr Chen Xiongzhang, vice president of Nanning University of Guangxi well deserve my gratitude for their ongoing concern as well as many useful suggestions.